PRIVATE

PILOT

SYLLABUS

JEPPESEN.
Sanderson Training Products

© Jeppesen Sanderson, Inc., 1997, 1998, 1999, 2000
All Rights Reserved
55 Inverness Drive East, Englewood, CO 80112-5498
ISBN 0-88487-240-8

PREFACE

The *Private Pilot Syllabus* has been specifically developed to meet the requirements of Title 14 CFR, Part 141. The syllabus should be considered as an abstract or digest of the course of training. As such, it is important that instructors also refer to the pertinent sections of the regulations during the conduct of the course. This will ensure that all aeronautical knowledge areas, flight proficiency, and experience requirements have been included during flight training and are documented in appropriate records. The terminology for maneuvers and procedures listed in the syllabus is aligned with the "tasks" which are published in the FAA's *Private Pilot Practical Test Standards*.

The syllabus has separate ground and flight training courses which are taught concurrently. The ground training syllabus is divided into three stages and contains a total of 17 ground lessons. The flight training syllabus also is divided into three stages and contains a total of 26 flight lessons. A stage check is shown at the end of each stage of flight training, and a stage exam is shown at the end of each stage of ground training. A presolo written exam is included before the first supervised solo. In addition, end-of-course knowledge tests and an end-of-course flight check are included in the syllabus prior to the conclusion of the respective ground and flight segments. The End-of-Course Flight Check is completed at the end of Stage III. The applicant must complete, or receive credit for, all of the ground and flight lessons in the *Private Pilot Syllabus*.

In concert with long-standing recommendations by both government and the general aviation industry, technological advances, such as computer-aided training, are incorporated into this syllabus. Use of a Personal Computer-Based Aviation Training Device (PCATD) for introductory and skill enhancement purposes is recommended for specified ground lessons. Use of the *Private Pilot Maneuvers Multimedia Training* also is recommended. Operators who wish to utilize either or both of these options should check the appropriate box(es) when they apply for Training Course Outline (TCO) approval. The student copy of the syllabus also should be marked accordingly.

❏ **This Syllabus utilizes a PCATD in the ground training segment.**

❏ **This Syllabus utilizes *Private Pilot Maneuvers Multimedia Training* for student training.**

PATRICK E BUCKLEY _____ is enrolled in the:
(Student's Name)

TABLE OF CONTENTS

PRIVATE PILOT COURSE INTRODUCTION

This syllabus utilizes the building-block theory of learning, which recognizes that each item taught must be presented on the basis of previously learned knowledge and skills. It is designed so the academic support materials can be coordinated with the flight lessons. When the coordinated sequence is used, the material pertinent to a flight lesson is taught just before the flight.

COURSE ELEMENTS

The Private Pilot Course contains separate ground and flight segments. Therefore, the course may be conducted as a combined ground and flight training program, or it may be divided into separate components. Regardless of the method used, the course includes the latest FAA pilot certification requirements and a maximum of student-oriented instruction. The syllabus and support materials not only provide necessary information, but also guide the student through the course in a logical manner.

GROUND TRAINING

In accordance with FAR Part 141, ground school training is an integral part of pilot certification courses. The ground training syllabus has been designed to meet this requirement and may be conducted concurrently with flight training or used as a separate ground training course.

If the ground school is coordinated with flight training, each ground lesson is conducted at the point indicated in the Lesson Time Allocation tables beginning on page XVI. This coordinated sequence is the most effective method for course utilization, because the academic knowledge is obtained immediately prior to its application during flight training.

As indicated in the Lesson Time Allocation tables, ground training Stages I and II are completed during Stage I of the flight training portion of the syllabus. Ground Stage III, and the end-of-course knowledge tests (Final Exams "A" and "B") are completed during Stage II of flight training. This permits the student to complete the academic segments of the syllabus early, before the final stage of flight training, and it encourages the student to take the FAA Airmen Knowledge Test at an opportune time.

When the course is presented in a classroom environment, lessons should be followed in numerical order as listed in the ground training segment of the syllabus. However, to provide a degree of flexibility for adapting to individual student needs and the training situation, the syllabus lessons may be altered with approval of the chief flight instructor. Any deviation should not disturb the course continuity or objective. Each lesson may be presented in one classroom session, or it may be divided into two or more sessions, as necessary.

USING THE GROUND LESSONS

Ground lessons are based on the Jeppesen Guided Flight Discovery (GFD) Pilot Training System. Although each component of the GFD Pilot Training System may be used separately, the effectiveness of the materials is maximized by using all of the individual elements together in an organized systems approach as described in this syllabus. The syllabus contains cross-references which direct the user to the appropriate GFD study materials for each lesson.

The ground lessons generally are divided into three sections — Lesson Introduction, Video Presentation, and Class Discussion. During the introduction, the instructor should outline the subject material to be covered during the training session, the objective for learning that information, and the performance standards necessary for successful lesson completion. Each ground lesson also includes Study Assignments for the next lesson. The main components of the Private Pilot GFD Program are described below.

TEXTBOOK

Prior to each ground lesson, the student should read and study the assigned *Private Pilot Manual* sections or chapter. This is the primary source for initial study and review. The text contains concise explanations of the fundamental concepts and ideas and is organized in a logical building-block sequence. Subjects often are expanded upon through the use of Discovery Insets which are strategically placed throughout the chapters. Periodically, human factors principles are presented in Human Element Insets which help explain how the mind and body function during flight. Throughout the manual, concepts which directly relate to FAA test questions are highlighted by FAA Question Insets. Key terms are highlighted in red throughout the text and a complete list is included at the end of each section. Summary Checklists and Questions are also included at the end of each section.

FAR/AIM CD-ROM

The *Private Pilot Manual* also contains a FAR/AIM CD-ROM. Federal Aviation Regulations (FARs) covered on the CD-ROM include Parts 1, 43, 61, 67, 71, 73, 91, 97, 119, 125, 133, 135, 141, 142, HMR 175, and NTSB 830. FAR Study Lists, along with FAR Exercises (and answers) also are included. The *Aeronautical Information Manual* (AIM) segment consists of the complete AIM with color graphics and the entire Pilot/Controller Glossary.

FLITESCHOOL CD-ROM

Private pilot knowledge areas also are covered in the FliteSchool multimedia software. These computer-based programs are organized into easy-to-study lessons that correspond to the chapters and sections in the *Private Pilot Manual*. This provides students with an alternative study method to accommodate individual needs and learning styles. Since FliteSchool is primarily intended for self-study, its use is recommended, but not required.

PRIVATE PILOT MANEUVERS

Three components provide for student introduction, study, and review. They are the *Private Pilot Maneuvers* manual, the *Private Pilot Maneuvers Multimedia Training*, and the *Maneuvers Videos*.

Private Pilot Maneuvers contains full color graphics and step-by-step procedural descriptions to help students visualize and understand each maneuver they will perform in the airplane. Additional guidance is provided through highlighted text which includes helpful hints, common errors, and FAA practical test standards.

Private Pilot Maneuvers Multimedia Training describes each maneuver using art, video, and animation on five interactive CD-ROMs. An instructor guides students through the maneuvers step-by-step, providing tips on improving performance and enhancing flying skills. The multimedia training also provides FAA practical test standards, as well as examines safety and human factors issues which apply to each maneuver. The CD-ROMs are suited to individual training, as well as classroom instruction.

The *Maneuvers Videos* present each maneuver or procedure from the student's perspective. The student can easily visualize how a maneuver looks from inside or outside the airplane. This simplifies the introduction of new maneuvers in the airplane.

Although maneuvers study assignments are included in the flight training section of the syllabus, specific time indicated in the Lesson Time Allocation Table may be credited toward total ground training time. The CD-ROMs are appropriate for out-of-class study and may be assigned accordingly. Formal class lesson times may be varied to fit individual student needs as long as the overall training time adds up to the required number of hours. For example, a given lesson, which may have one hour allocated for multimedia training, video, and discussion, may be reorganized, shortened, or extended as necessary to accomplish the desired training.

VIDEO PRESENTATIONS

Video presentations provide an overview of the major knowledge areas in the *Private Pilot Manual*. During the video presentation, the students should be encouraged to ask questions and obtain clarification of subject material, as necessary. After the students have viewed the material, the instructor conducts a discussion session. The purpose of the discussion is to elaborate upon the subject material and answer any questions the students may have.

QUESTIONS

One of the final steps during a typical ground lesson is completion of the questions assigned at the end of each textbook section. Any incorrect responses should be discussed. This ensures student understanding of the subject material prior to beginning the next ground lesson. When the lesson is complete, the instructor assigns the next chapter and corresponding CD-ROM for out-of-class study.

USING THE PCATD

The syllabus also provides for use of a Personal Computer-Based Aviation Training Device (PCATD) in the private pilot ground training course. A PCATD can assist an instructor in achieving specific instructional objectives by introducing the procedural aspects of flight training in a ground training phase. If properly integrated into the ground training program, the PCATD will enhance systems knowledge and procedural understanding by the applicant before engaging in flight training in the airplane. **No flight training credit for the PCATD is permitted for a private pilot course.**

In addition to skill enhancement, the introduction of maneuvers and procedures by instrument reference in the PCATD has other advantages for both student and instructor. These include fewer distractions, more versatility in lesson presentation, repositioning, freeze functions, emergency training, and the ability to control the environment of the training session and allow the student to concentrate on the areas the instructor wants to emphasize. By following the recommended sequence of the syllabus, the student will gain maximum benefit from the integration of academic training, introduction of new maneuvers and procedures in the PCATD, and subsequent practice in the airplane.

As indicated on the Preface page, if the box for PCATD utilization is checked, then the PCATD becomes part of the ground training segments for the approved course, and use of the PCATD is required. If the box for PCATD is left blank, the PCATD is not part of the approved course, and its use is not required.

PCATD utilization should be flexible in a private pilot ground training course. The accompanying table shows the recommended ground lessons where PCATD training can be highly effective.

PCATD GROUND LESSONS

Ground Lesson 1 — Introduction to Aviation (1 Hour)
Ground Lesson 2 — Airplane Systems (1 Hour)
Ground Lesson 5 — Communications (1 Hour)
Ground Lesson 12 — Navigation (1 Hour)
Ground Lesson 14 — Flying the Cross-Country (1 Hour)

Additional information on use of a PCATD is contained in the Instructor's Support chapter of the *Instructor's Guide*. PCATD lesson plans are included.

STAGE EXAMS

The ground training portion of the syllabus includes three lessons specifically devoted to Stage Exams. These are ground lessons 6, 10, and 15. The intent of the Stage Exam is to evaluate the student's understanding of the knowledge areas within a stage. Successful completion of each Stage Exam and a review of each incorrect response is required before the student progresses to the next stage.

FINAL EXAMS

When all of the ground lesson assignments are complete, the student should take the private end-of-course knowledge exams. According to the syllabus, lessons 16 and 17 for these end-of-course exams are completed in Stage II. The Private Pilot Final Exam "A" is administered first in ground lesson 16. Private Pilot Final Exam "B," which is ground lesson 17, serves as the ground training course final examination. Following the test, the instructor should assign each student appropriate subject areas for review. After a thorough review, the actual FAA airmen knowledge test should be completed without delay.

FLIGHT TRAINING

The flight training syllabus also is divided into three stages, each providing an important segment of pilot training. Each stage builds on previous learning and, therefore, should be completed in sequence. However, to provide a degree of flexibility for adapting to individual student needs and the training environment, the syllabus lessons may be altered with approval of the chief flight instructor. Any deviation should not disturb the course continuity or objective. The following discussion presents a description of the primary areas of study in each stage.

STAGE I

Stage I of the syllabus is designed to provide a strong foundation prior to the first solo flight. In this stage, the basic maneuvers are introduced, practiced, and reviewed. The student develops the knowledge, skill, and habit patterns needed for solo flight. In addition, the student will practice airport operations, different types of takeoffs and landings, emergency procedures, and ground reference maneuvers. This stage also includes a thorough review of previously learned maneuvers. During this stage, the student must complete the presolo written exam and briefing prior to the first solo flight. Guidance on administering the presolo written exam is provided by AC 61-101, *Presolo Written Test*, and additional information is included in the *Instructor's Guide* chapter containing the Pilot Briefings.

Instructors also should review pertinent sections of FAR Part 61. For example, 61.87(d) contains specific maneuvers and procedures for the presolo phase of training. Although the terminology for some of these maneuvers and procedures differs somewhat from Part 141 and PTS terminology, it is important to ensure compliance with all presolo training requirements specified in Part 61.

STAGE II

The advanced maneuvers portion of this stage is designed to introduce short-field and soft-field takeoffs and climbs, approaches, landings, radio navigation, and unimproved airport operations, as well as flight by reference to instruments and night flying. The maneuvers introduced during this stage incorporate the skills developed during Stage I, and are important to the cross-country operations later in this stage.

The cross-country portion of this stage provides the necessary information, knowledge, and skills so the student may begin cross-country operations. With the knowledge acquired during Stage II, the student should be able to safely conduct solo cross-country flights. Proficiency in advanced maneuvers and cross-country procedures will be evaluated during the stage check in Flight 20.

STAGE III

The flights of Stage III are designed to provide the student with the proficiency required for the private pilot practical test. These flights are devoted to gaining experience and confidence in cross-country operations and reviewing all maneuvers within the syllabus to attain maximum pilot proficiency. The student's proficiency and knowledge will be checked by the chief flight instructor, assistant chief instructor, or check instructor during the Stage Check in Flight 25, and further review may be pursued as necessary.

PREFLIGHT ORIENTATION

Prior to each dual and solo flight, the instructor must provide the student with an overview of the subject matter to be covered during the lesson. The instructor should select a quiet, private place to brief the student and explain the lesson subject matter. It is important that the instructor define unfamiliar terms, explain the maneuvers and objectives of each lesson, and discuss human factors concepts related to each lesson.

Each Flight Lesson contains Preflight Discussion information which is intended to provide a basis for the instructor's preflight overview. This overview should be flexible; these are only suggested topics. Every item does not need to be covered. The

preflight orientation should be tailored to the specific flight, the local environment, and especially for the benefit of the individual student.

FLIGHT SIMULATOR OR FTD

If the flight school incorporates the use of a flight simulator or flight training device (FTD) in the private pilot training program, the syllabus allows for the instruction in simulator or FTD sessions. Training in a simulator that meets the requirements of 141.41(a) may be credited for a maximum of 20 percent of the total flight training hour requirements (20% × 35 hours = 7.0 hours). Training in an FTD that meets the requirements of 141.41(b) may be credited for a maximum of 15 percent of the total flight training hour requirements (15% × 35 hours = 5.25 hours).

AIRPLANE PRACTICE

Airplane practice must be conducted so that the student obtains the maximum benefit from each flight. Each flight should begin with a review of previously learned maneuvers before any new maneuvers are introduced.

Prior to each solo flight, the instructor should carefully instruct the student in the maneuvers to be performed during the flight and what is to be accomplished. This guidance will ensure that the student receives maximum benefit from the solo flight.

POSTFLIGHT EVALUATION

The postflight evaluation is at least as important as the preflight orientation. During each postflight session, the student must be debriefed thoroughly. Noticeable advancement should be apparent and recommendations should be made for improvement, where appropriate. This action is a valuable instructional technique because it increases retention and, to some degree, prepares the student for the next lesson.

As a guide, a minimum of one-half hour per flight is recommended for preflight and postflight briefings combined. Note that this reflects the time spent with the well-prepared student. If necessary, additional time should be allotted.

STUDENT STAGE CHECKS

Stage checks measure the student's accomplishments during each stage of training. The conduct of each stage check is the responsibility of the chief flight instructor. However, the chief instructor may delegate authority for conducting stage checks and end-of-course tests to the assistant chief instructor or the designated check instructor. This procedure provides close supervision of training and may provide another opinion on the student's progress. The stage check also gives the chief instructor an opportunity to check the effectiveness of the instructors.

An examination of the building-block theory of learning will show that it is extremely important for progress and proficiency to be satisfactory before the student enters a new stage of training. Therefore, the next stage should not begin until the student successfully completes the stage check. Failure to follow this progression may defeat the purpose of the stage check and degrade the overall effectiveness of the course.

Pilot Briefings

Three Pilot Briefings are also integrated into the flight syllabus. They are:
1. Presolo Written Exam and Briefing
2. Solo Cross-Country Briefing
3. Private Pilot Practical Test Briefing

Pilot Briefing material is located in the *Instructor's Guide*. Each briefing consists of a series of questions which provide comprehensive coverage of the pertinent information. Answers, when applicable, are included. The student should be provided with the questions (not the answers) in advance of the actual briefing. In this way, the student can research the questions and gain optimum benefit from the briefing.

The briefings should be conducted as private tutoring sessions to test each student's comprehension. Due to their importance, these briefings should be held in a comfortable classroom or office environment, and ample time should be scheduled. Every question should be discussed thoroughly to ensure the student understands the key points. The briefings are to be completed during the preflight orientation for the appropriate flight. Correct placement of the briefings is indicated in the flight syllabus.

The Presolo Written Exam and Briefing is unique. As specified in FAR 61.87, a student must demonstrate satisfactory knowledge of the required subject areas by completing a written exam. This exam is to be administered and graded by the instructor who endorses the student pilot certificate for solo flight. As indicated in AC 61-101, Presolo Written Test, flight instructors must include questions on applicable portions of FAR Parts 61 and 91. In addition, instructors should modify the written exam as necessary to make it appropriate for the aircraft to be flown and the local flying environment.

FAR PART 61 OPERATION

The *Private Pilot Syllabus* is designed to meet all the requirements of FAR Part 141, Appendix B, and also may be adapted to meet the aeronautical knowledge, proficiency, and experience (airplane, single-engine) requirements of FAR Part 61. See FAR 61.105, 61.107, and 61.109. The basic difference between the flight time requirements of Part 141 and Part 61 is that under Part 61, the student must have at least 40 hours of flight time that includes at least 20 hours of flight instruction from an authorized instructor and 10 hours of solo flight training (in specified areas of operation). The flight time requirements of Part 141 are nearly the same, except total flight time is only 35 hours. Adapting this syllabus to Part 61 training requires only a slight modification of individual flight lesson times.

The ground training requirements under Part 61 specify that an applicant for a knowledge test is required to have a logbook endorsement from an authorized instructor who conducted the training or reviewed the person's home study course. The endorsement must indicate satisfactory completion of the ground instruction or home study course required for the certificate or rating sought. A home study course for the purposes of FAR Part 61 is a course of study in those aeronautical knowledge areas specified in FAR 61.105, and organized by a pilot school, publisher, flight or ground instructor, or by the student. The Private Pilot Course easily meets this requirement. As a practical consideration, students seeking pilot certification under FAR Part 61 should receive some formal ground training, either in the classroom or from an authorized flight or ground instructor.

CREDIT FOR PREVIOUS TRAINING

According to FAR 141.77, when a student transfers from one FAA-approved school to another approved school, course credits obtained in the previous course of training may be credited for 50 percent of the curriculum requirements by the receiving school. However, the receiving school must determine the amount of credit to be allowed based upon a proficiency test or knowledge test, or both, conducted by the receiving school. A student who enrolls in a course of training may receive credit for 25 percent of the curriculum requirements for knowledge and experience gained in a non-Part 141 flight school, and the credit must be based upon a proficiency test or knowledge test, or both, conducted by the receiving school. The amount of credit for previous training allowed, whether received from an FAA-approved school or other source, is determined by the receiving school. In addition, the previous provider of the training must certify the kind and amount of training given, and the result of each stage check and end-of-course test, if applicable.

COURSE OVERVIEW — GROUND TRAINING

Completion of this course is based solely upon compliance with the minimum requirements of FAR Part 141. The accompanying tables with times shown in hours are provided mainly for guidance in achieving regulatory compliance.

PRIVATE PILOT CERTIFICATION COURSE
AIRPLANE SINGLE-ENGINE LAND

GROUND TRAINING						
	Private Pilot Maneuvers Class Discussion, Video, and CD-ROM	PCATD	Private Pilot Manual Class Discussion, and Video	Pilot Briefings	Stage/ Final Exams	Exam Debriefings
GROUND STAGE I	3.0	3.0	10.0		1.0	As Required
GROUND STAGE II	3.0		6.0	2.0	1.0	As Required
GROUND STAGE III	3.0	2.0	8.0	2.0	4.0	1.0
TOTALS	9.0	5.0	24.0	4.0	6.0	1.0

NOTE:
1. The first column shows the recommended *Private Pilot Maneuvers* discussion, video, and/or CD-ROM training time.
2. The second column shows the maximum PCATD training time when a PCATD is part of the approved course.
3. The third column shows the minimum recommended training time for *Private Pilot Manual* class discussion, and video. Times shown in columns 1 and 2 may be credited toward the total time shown in column 3 as follows:
   • Up to 9 hours of Private Pilot Maneuvers class discussion, video, and/or CD-ROM and/or
   • Up to 5 hours of PCATD training.
To recieve credit for CD-ROM and/or PCATD training time, the associated course approval must be obtained (See Preface)

COURSE OVERVIEW — FLIGHT TRAINING

FLIGHT TRAINING

	DUAL					SOLO		
	Day Local	Day Cross Country	Night Local	Night Cross Country	Instrument	Day Local	Cross Country	Dual/Solo Combined Totals
FLIGHT STAGE I	9.0				(1.0)	.5		9.5
FLIGHT STAGE II	4.0	2.0	1.0	2.0	(2.0)	2.0	2.5	13.5
FLIGHT STAGE III	6.0						6.0	12.0
TOTALS	19.0	2.0	1.0	2.0	(3.0)	2.5	8.5	35.0

NOTE: 1. Dual instrument training in the airplane is allocated to portions of flight lessons 3, 4, 5, 7, 8, 14, 15, 17, and 18 for a total of 3.0 hours. The minimum recommended times are .2 hours (12 minutes) each for Flight Lesson 3, 4, 5, 7, and 8 and .5 hours (30 minutes) each for Flight Lessons 14, 15, 17, and 18. The total of 3.0 hours of instrument training is specified in Appendix B, Part 141.

       2. For the purpose of meeting cross-country time requirements for a private pilot certificate, a landing must be accomplished at least a straight-line distance of more than 50 nautical miles from the original point of departure.

LESSON TIME ALLOCATION

Private Pilot Maneuvers discussion, video, and/or CD-ROM	PCATD	Private Pilot Manual class discussion, and video	Pilot Briefings	Stage/Final Exams	Exam Debriefings		Dual Day Local	Dual Day Cross-Country	Dual Night Local	Dual Night Cross-Country	Dual Instrument	Solo Day Local	Solo Cross-Country	
						GROUND STAGE I, II AND FLIGHT STAGE I								
	1.0	2.0				Ground Lesson 1 – Discovering Aviation								
	1.0	2.0				Ground Lesson 2 – Airplane Systems								
						Flight 1	.5							→
		2.0				Ground Lesson 3 – Aerodynamic Principles								
1.0						Flight 2	1.0							→
		2.0				Ground Lesson 4 – The Flight Environment								
1.0						Flight 3	1.0				(.2)			→
	1.0	2.0				Ground Lesson 5 – Communication & Flight Info.								
1.0						Flight 4	1.0				(.2)			→
				1.0	As Req.	Ground Lesson 6 – Stage I Exam								
1.0						Flight 5	1.0				(.2)			→
		2.0				Ground Lesson 7 – Meteorology for Pilots								
1.0						Flight 6	1.0							→
		2.0				Ground Lesson 8 – Federal Aviation Regulations								
1.0						Flight 7	1.0				(.2)			→
		2.0				Ground Lesson 9 – Interpreting Weather Data								
			2.0		As Req.	Presolo Written Exam and Briefing								
						Flight 8	1.0				(.2)			→
						Flight 9	.5					.5		→
				1.0	As Req.	Ground Lesson 10 – Stage II Exam								
						Flight 10 – Stage Check	1.0							
6.0	3.0	16.0	2.0	2.0	As Req.	Stage Totals	9.0				(1.0)	.5		

NOTE: 1. The first column shows the recommended *Private Pilot Maneuvers* discussion, video, and/or CD-ROM training time.
2. The second column shows the maximum PCATD training time when a PCATD is part of the approved course.
3. The third column shows the minimum recommended training time for *Private Pilot Manual* class discussion, and video. Times shown in columns 1 and 2 may be credited toward the total time shown in column 3 as follows:
   • Up to 9 hours of *Private Pilot Maneuvers* class discussion, video, and/or CD-ROM and/or
   • Up to 5 hours of PCATD training.
To recieve credit for CD-ROM and/or PCATD training time, the associated course approval must be obtained (See Preface)

LESSON TIME ALLOCATION

Ground Training							Flight Training — Dual					Solo	
Private Pilot Maneuvers discussion, video, and/or CD-ROM	PCATD	Private Pilot Manual class discussion, and video	Pilot Briefings	Stage/Final Exams	Exam Debriefings		Day Local	Day Cross-Country	Night Local	Night Cross-Country	Instrument	Day Local	Cross-Country
GROUND STAGE III AND FLIGHT STAGE II													
		2.0				Ground Lesson 11 – Airplane Performance							
1.0						Flight 11	1.0						
	1.0	2.0				Ground Lesson 12 – Navigation							
						Flight 12					1.0		
		2.0				Ground Lesson 13 – Human Factor Principles							
						Flight 13					1.0		
	1.0	2.0				Ground Lesson 14 – Flying Cross Country							
1.0						Flight 14	1.0					(.5)	
				1.0	As Req.	Ground Lesson 15 – Stage III Exam							
						Flight 15	1.0					(.5)	
						Flight 16			1.0				
1.0						Flight 17		2.0				(.5)	
						Flight 18				2.0		(.5)	
			2.0			Briefing – Solo Cross-Country							
						Flight 19							2.5
				3.0	1.0	Ground Lesson 16 & 17 – Final Exams A & B							
						Flight 20 – Stage Check	1.0						
3.0	2.0	8.0	2.0	4.0	1.0	**Stage Totals**	4.0	2.0	1.0	2.0	(2.0)	2.0	2.5

NOTE:
1. The first column shows the recommended *Private Pilot Maneuvers* discussion, video, and/or CD-ROM training time.
2. The second column shows the maximum PCATD training time when a PCATD is part of the approved course.
3. The third column shows the minimum recommended training time for *Private Pilot Manual* class discussion, and video. Times shown in columns 1 and 2 may be credited toward the total time shown in column 3 as follows:
   - Up to 9 hours of *Private Pilot Maneuvers* class discussion, video, and/or CD-ROM and/or
   - Up to 5 hours of PCATD training.

To recieve credit for CD-ROM and/or PCATD training time, the associated course approval must be obtained (See Preface)

LESSON TIME ALLOCATION

Private Pilot Maneuvers discussion, video, and/or CD-ROM	PCATD	Private Pilot Manual class discussion, and video	Pilot Briefings	Stage/Final Exams	Exam Debriefings		Day Local	Day Cross-Country	Night Local	Night Cross-Country	Instrument	Day Local	Cross-Country
						Ground Training / **Flight Training** **Dual** / **Solo**							
						FLIGHT STAGE III							
						Flight 21							2.0
						Flight 22							4.0
						Flight 23	2.0				As Req.		
						Flight 24	2.0				As Req.		
						Flight 25 – Stage Check	1.0						
			As Req.			Briefing – Private Pilot Practical Test							
						Flight 26 – End-of-Course Flight Check	1.0				As Req.		
						Stage Totals	6.0					2.0	6.0
9.0	5.0	24.0	4.0	6.0	1.0	Private Pilot Course – Overall Totals	19.0	2.0	1.0	2.0	(3.0)	2.5	8.5

The individual times shown on the accompanying Lesson Time Allocation tables are for instructor/student guidance only; they are not mandatory for each ground lesson, flight, or stage of training. At the conclusion of this course, the student must meet the minimum requirements of FAR Part 141, Appendix B, for each catagory in order to graduate. Preflight and postflight briefing times are not specified, but a minimum of .5 hours for each dual and solo flight is suggested. The times for Pilot Briefings, although assigned and completed along with selected flight lessons, are considered part of ground training.

PRIVATE PILOT SYLLABUS INTRODUCTION

The Guided Flight Discovery (GFD) Training System is designed to coordinate the academic study assignments and flight training required by pilots operating in an increasingly complex aviation environment. New subject matter is introduced during the ground lessons with multimedia formats, including the following:

1. In-depth textbook assignments and question material — *Private Pilot Manual, Private Pilot Maneuvers*

2. *Private Pilot Maneuvers Multimedia Training*

3. Video presentations

4. Thorough instructor/student discussions

5. Stage and end-of-course exams for evaluation and reinforcement

6. PCATD introductory/skill enhancement lessons

For optimum effectiveness, ground lessons should be completed just prior to the respective flight lessons, as outlined in the syllabus. However, it is also acceptable to present lessons in a formal ground school before the student is introduced to the airplane. If a considerable length of time has elapsed between the ground lesson and the associated flight, the instructor may wish to conduct a short review of essential material. One rule dictated by sound educational philosophy is that the flight lesson should not be conducted until the related ground lesson has been completed.

In selected flight lessons, the abbreviation "VR" is used to indicate that students should maintain aircraft control by using visual reference. "IR" indicates that instrument reference should be used. No reference, to either "VR" or "IR," indicates normal private pilot maneuvers or procedures by visual references.

PRIVATE PILOT
CERTIFICATION COURSE
AIRPLANE
SINGLE-ENGINE LAND

Course Objectives — The student will obtain the knowledge, skill, and aeronautical experience necessary to meet the requirements for a private pilot certificate with an airplane category rating and a single-engine land class rating.

Course Completion Standards — The student must demonstrate through knowledge tests, flight tests, and show through appropriate records that he/she meets the knowledge, skill, and experience requirements necessary to obtain a private pilot certificate with an airplane category rating and a single-engine land class rating.

STUDENT INFORMATION
COURSE ENROLLMENT
There are no specific prerequisites for initial enrollment in the ground portion of the ◄───── course and beginning your training. However, a person must hold a recreational or student pilot certificate prior to enrolling in the flight portion of a private pilot certification course.

REQUIREMENTS FOR SOLO FLIGHT
Before you can fly solo, you must hold a student pilot certificate and at least a current third-class medical certificate. You also must be at least 16 years of age in order to obtain a student pilot certificate and be able to read, speak, write, and understand the English language. Remember that solo flight operations require specific training, successful completion of a presolo written exam, and endorsements from your flight instructor.

REQUIREMENTS FOR GRADUATION
You must be at least 17 years of age to graduate, be able to read, speak, write, and understand the English language, meet the same requirements listed in the time table for dual and solo flight, and satisfactorily complete the training outlined in this syllabus. When you meet the minimum requirements of FAR Part 141, Appendix B, you may be considered eligible for graduation.

LESSON DESCRIPTION AND STAGES OF TRAINING
Each lesson is fully described within the syllabus, including the objectives, standards, and measurable units of accomplishment and learning. The stage objectives and standards are described at the beginning of each stage within the syllabus.

TESTS AND CHECKS

The syllabus incorporates stage checks and end-of-course tests in accordance with FAR 141, Appendix B. The chief instructor is responsible for ensuring that each student accomplishes the required stage checks and end-of-course tests in accordance with the school's approved training course. However, the chief instructor may delegate authority for stage checks and end-of-course tests to the assistant chief or check instructor. You also must complete stage exams, pilot briefings, and final examinations that are described within the syllabus. In addition, you must satisfactorily accomplish a final test after all of the stages have been completed in accordance with Part 141, Appendix B.

Private Pilot Ground Training Syllabus

Ground Training Course Objectives

The student will obtain the necessary aeronautical knowledge and meet the prerequisites specified in FAR Part 61 for a private pilot airmen knowledge test.

Ground Training Completion Standards

The student will demonstrate through practical and knowledge tests, and records, that he/she meets the prerequisites specified in FAR Part 61, and has the knowledge necessary to pass the private pilot airmen knowledge test.

Stage I

Stage Objectives

During this stage, the student will be introduced to pilot training, aviation opportunities, human factors in aviation, and become familiar with airplane systems and ◄—— aerodynamic principles, as well as the flight environment. The student also will obtain a basic knowledge of safety of flight, airports, aeronautical charts, airspace, radio communications, and air traffic control services, including the use of radar. In addition, the student will learn radio procedures and the common sources of flight information.

Stage Completion Standards

This stage is complete when the student has completed the Stage I written exam with a minimum passing score of 80%, and the instructor has reviewed each incorrect response to ensure complete understanding before the student progresses to Stage II.

STAGE I
GROUND LESSON 1

LESSON REFERENCES:

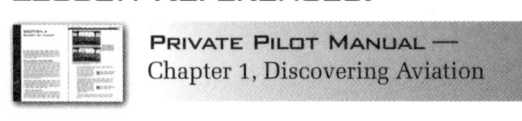

PRIVATE PILOT MANUAL —
Chapter 1, Discovering Aviation

RECOMMENDED SEQUENCE:

NOTE: *Students should read Chapter 1, Sections A, B, and C, prior to Ground Lesson 1.*

1. Lesson Introduction
2. Class Discussion
3. PCATD

LESSON OBJECTIVES:

- Become familiar with pilot training, aviation opportunities, and human factors in aviation.
- Gain a basic understanding of the school's pilot training program.

ACADEMIC CONTENT:

SECTION A — PILOT TRAINING
- ❏ How to Get Started
- ❏ Role of the FAA
- ❏ Fixed-Base Operators (FBOs)
- ❏ Eligibility Requirements
- ❏ Types of Training Available
- ❏ Phases of Training
- ❏ Private Pilot Privileges and Limitations

SECTION B — AVIATION OPPORTUNITIES
- ❏ New Experiences
- ❏ Aviation Organizations
- ❏ Category/Class Ratings
- ❏ Additional Pilot Certificates
- ❏ Aviation Careers

SECTION C — INTRODUCTION TO HUMAN FACTORS
- ❏ Aeronautical Decision Making
- ❏ Crew Resource Management Training
- ❏ Pilot in Command Responsibility

- Communication
- Resource Use
- Workload Management
- Situational Awareness
- Aviation Physiology
- Alcohol, Drugs, and Performance
- Fitness for Flight

STUDY ASSIGNMENT:

 PRIVATE PILOT MANUAL —
Chapter 2, Airplane Systems

COMPLETION STANDARDS:

The student will indicate, through oral quizzing, familiarity with pilot training programs, opportunities in aviation, and human factors. In addition, the instructor will make sure the student has a basic understanding of policies and procedures applicable to the school's pilot training program.

STAGE I
GROUND LESSON 2

LESSON REFERENCES:

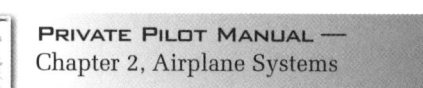 PRIVATE PILOT MANUAL —
Chapter 2, Airplane Systems

 PART I, CHAPTER 2

RECOMMENDED SEQUENCE:
1. Lesson Introduction and Video Presentation
2. Class Discussion
3. PCATD

LESSON OBJECTIVES:
• Gain a basic understanding of the main airplane components and systems.
• Become familiar with flight instrument functions and operating characteristics, including errors and common malfunctions.
• Learn about the powerplant and related systems.

ACADEMIC CONTENT:
SECTION A — AIRPLANES
❏ Fuselage
❏ Wings
❏ Empennage
❏ Landing Gear
❏ Engine/Propeller
❏ Pilot's Operating Handbook (POH)

SECTION B — THE POWERPLANT AND RELATED SYSTEMS
❏ Reciprocating Engine
❏ Induction Systems
❏ Supercharging and Turbocharging
❏ Ignition Systems
❏ Fuel Systems
❏ Refueling
❏ Oil Systems
❏ Cooling Systems
❏ Exhaust Systems

- ❑ Propellers
- ❑ Propeller Hazards
- ❑ Electrical Systems

SECTION C — FLIGHT INSTRUMENTS
- ❑ Pitot-Static Instruments
- ❑ Airspeed Indicator
- ❑ Altimeter
- ❑ Vertical Speed Indicator
- ❑ Gyroscopic Instruments
- ❑ Magnetic Compass

STUDY ASSIGNMENT:

 PRIVATE PILOT MANUAL —
Chapter 3, Aerodynamic Principles

COMPLETION STANDARDS:

- Demonstrate understanding during oral quizzing by instructor at completion of lesson.
- Student completes Chapter 2 questions for Sections A, B, and C with a minimum passing score of 80%. Instructor reviews incorrect responses to ensure complete student understanding prior to progression to Ground Lesson 3.

STAGE I
GROUND LESSON 3

LESSON REFERENCES:

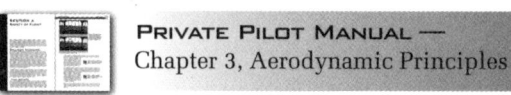

PRIVATE PILOT MANUAL —
Chapter 3, Aerodynamic Principles

PART I, CHAPTER 3

RECOMMENDED SEQUENCE:
1. Lesson Introduction and Video Presentation
2. Class Discussion

LESSON OBJECTIVES:
- Become familiar with the four forces of flight, aerodynamic principles of stability, maneuvering flight, and load factor.
- Gain a basic understanding of stall/spin characteristics as they relate to training airplanes.
- Learn the importance of prompt recognition of stall indications.

ACADEMIC CONTENT:
SECTION A — FOUR FORCES OF FLIGHT
- [ ] Lift
- [ ] Airfoils
- [ ] Pilot Control of Lift
- [ ] Weight
- [ ] Thrust
- [ ] Drag
- [ ] Ground Effect

SECTION B — STABILITY
- [ ] Three Axes of Flight
- [ ] Longitudinal Stability
- [ ] Center of Gravity Position
- [ ] Lateral Stability
- [ ] Directional Stability
- [ ] Stalls
- [ ] Spins

❑ Climbing Flight
❑ Left-Turning Tendencies
❑ Descending Flight
❑ Turning Flight
❑ Load Factor

STUDY ASSIGNMENT:

PRIVATE PILOT MANUAL —
Chapter 4, The Flight Environment

COMPLETION STANDARDS:

- Demonstrate understanding during oral quizzing by instructor at completion of lesson.
- Student completes Chapter 3 questions for Sections A, B, and C with a minimum passing score of 80%. Instructor reviews incorrect responses to ensure complete student understanding prior to progression to Ground Lesson 4.

STAGE I
GROUND LESSON 4

LESSON REFERENCES:

 **PRIVATE PILOT MANUAL —**
Chapter 4, The Flight Environment

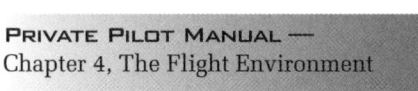 **PART II, CHAPTER 4**

RECOMMENDED SEQUENCE:
1. Lesson Introduction and Video Presentation
2. Class Discussion

LESSON OBJECTIVES:
- Understand important safety considerations, including collision avoidance precautions, right-of-way rules, and minimum safe altitudes.
- Become familiar with airport marking and lighting, aeronautical charts, and types of airspace.
- Learn about collision avoidance procedures and runway incursion avoidance.

ACADEMIC CONTENT:
SECTION A — SAFETY OF FLIGHT
❏ Collision Avoidance/Visual Scanning
❏ Airport Operations
❏ Right-of-Way Rules
❏ Minimum Safe Altitudes
❏ Taxiing in Wind
❏ Positive Exchange of Flight Controls

SECTION B — AIRPORTS
❏ Controlled and Uncontrolled
❏ Runway Layout
❏ Traffic Pattern
❏ Airport Visual Aids
❏ Taxiway Markings
❏ Ramp Area Hand Signals
❏ Runway Incursion Avoidance
❏ Land and Hold Short Operations (LAHSO)
❏ Airport Lighting
❏ Visual Glideslope Indicators   (7/99)

❑ Approach Light Systems
❑ Pilot-Controlled Lighting

SECTION C — AERONAUTICAL CHARTS
❑ Latitude and Longitude
❑ Projections
❑ Sectional Charts
❑ World Aeronautical Charts
❑ Chart Symbology

SECTION D — AIRSPACE
❑ Classifications
❑ Uncontrolled Airspace
❑ Controlled Airspace
❑ Class E
❑ Class D
❑ Class C
❑ Class B
❑ Class A
❑ Special VFR
❑ Special Use Airspace
❑ Other Airspace Areas
❑ Emergency Air Traffic Rules
❑ Air Defense Identification Zones

STUDY ASSIGNMENT:

 PRIVATE PILOT MANUAL — Chapter 5, Communication and Flight Information

COMPLETION STANDARDS:

- Demonstrate understanding during oral quizzing by instructor at completion of lesson.
- Student completes Chapter 4 questions for Sections A, B, C, and D with a minimum passing score of 80%. Instructor reviews incorrect responses to ensure complete student understanding prior to progression to Ground Lesson 5.

STAGE I
GROUND LESSON 5

LESSON REFERENCES:

 **PRIVATE PILOT MANUAL —**
Chapter 5, Communication and Flight Information

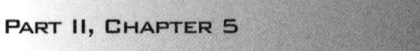 **PART II, CHAPTER 5**

RECOMMENDED SEQUENCE:
1. Lesson Introduction and Video Presentation
2. Class Discussion
3. PCATD

LESSON OBJECTIVES:
- Become familiar with radar, transponder operations, and FAA radar equipment and services for VFR aircraft.
- Understand the types of service provided by an FSS.
- Learn how to use the radio for communication.
- Gain a basic understanding of the sources of flight information, particularly the *Aeronautical Information Manual* and FAA advisory circulars.

ACADEMIC CONTENT:
SECTION A — RADAR AND ATC SERVICES
☑ Radar
☑ Transponder Operation
☑ FAA Radar Systems
☑ VFR Radar Services
☑ Automatic Terminal Information Service (ATIS)
☑ Flight Service Stations
☑ VHF Direction Finder Assistance

SECTION B — RADIO PROCEDURES

- ☑ VHF Communication Equipment
- ☑ Using the Radio
- ☑ Phonetic Alphabet
- ☑ Coordinated Universal Time
- ☑ Common Traffic Advisory Frequency (CTAF)
- ☑ ATC Facilities and Controlled Airports
- ☑ Lost Communication Procedures
- ☑ Emergency Procedures
- ☑ Emergency Locator Transmitters (ELTs)

SECTION C — SOURCES OF FLIGHT INFORMATION

- ☑ *Airport/Facility Directory*
- ☑ Federal Aviation Regulations
- ☑ *Aeronautical Information Manual* (AIM)
- ☑ Notices to Airmen (NOTAMs)
- ☑ Advisory Circulars
- ☑ Jeppesen Information Services

STUDY ASSIGNMENT:

PRIVATE PILOT MANUAL —
Review Chapters 2, 3, 4, and 5 in
preparation for the Stage I Exam.

COMPLETION STANDARDS:

- Demonstrate under-
  standing during oral
  quizzing by instructor
  at completion of lesson.
- Student completes
  Chapter 5 questions for
  Sections A, B, and C
  with a minimum pass-
  ing score of 80%.
  Instructor reviews
  incorrect responses to
  ensure complete stu-
  dent understanding
  prior to progression to
  the Stage Exam in
  Ground Lesson 6.

STAGE I
GROUND LESSON 6
Stage I Exam

LESSON REFERENCES:

 PRIVATE PILOT MANUAL —
Chapters 1 through 5

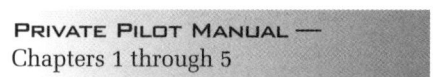 PART I AND II, CHAPTERS 1–5

RECOMMENDED SEQUENCE:
1. Lesson Introduction
2. Testing
3. Critique

LESSON OBJECTIVES:
- Demonstrate comprehension of the material presented in Chapters 1 through 5 of the *Private Pilot Manual*.

ACADEMIC CONTENT:
STAGE I EXAM
- ❏ Airplane Systems
- ❏ Aerodynamic Principles
- ❏ The Flight Environment
- ❏ Communication and Flight Information

STUDY ASSIGNMENT:

 PRIVATE PILOT MANUAL —
Chapter 6, Meteorology for Pilots

COMPLETION STANDARDS:

This lesson and stage are complete when the student has completed the Stage I Exam with a minimum of 80%, and the instructor has reviewed each incorrect response to ensure complete understanding before the student progresses to Stage II.

STAGE II

STAGE OBJECTIVES

During this stage, the student will become familiar with weather theory, typical weather patterns, and aviation weather hazards. In addition to meteorological theory, the student will learn how to obtain and interpret various weather reports, forecasts, and graphic charts. Finally, the student will become thoroughly familiar with FARs as they apply to private pilot operations.

STAGE COMPLETION STANDARDS

This stage is complete when the student has completed the Stage II written exam with a minimum passing score of 80%, and the instructor has reviewed each incorrect response to ensure complete understanding before the student progresses to Stage III.

STAGE II
GROUND LESSON 7

LESSON REFERENCES:

 **PRIVATE PILOT MANUAL —**
Chapter 6, Meteorology for Pilots

 **PART III, CHAPTER 6**

RECOMMENDED SEQUENCE:

1. Lesson Introduction and Video Presentation
2. Class Discussion

LESSON OBJECTIVES:

* Learn the causes of various weather conditions, frontal systems, and hazardous weather phenomena.
* Understand how to recognize critical weather situations from the ground and during flight, including hazards associated with thunderstorms.
* Become familiar with the recognition and avoidance of wind shear and wake turbulence.

ACADEMIC CONTENT:

SECTION A — BASIC WEATHER THEORY
❑ The Atmosphere
❑ Atmospheric Circulation
❑ Atmospheric Pressure
❑ Coriolis Force
❑ Global Wind Patterns
❑ Local Wind Patterns

SECTION B — WEATHER PATTERNS
❑ Atmospheric Stability
❑ Temperature Inversions
❑ Moisture
❑ Humidity
❑ Dewpoint
❑ Clouds and Fog
❑ Precipitation
❑ Airmasses

❏ Thunderstorms
❏ Turbulence
❏ Wake Turbulence
❏ Wind Shear
❏ Microburst
❏ Icing
❏ Restrictions to Visibility
❏ Volcanic Ash

STUDY ASSIGNMENT:

FAR/AIM OR FAR/AIM CD-ROM —
Private Pilot FARs, Recommended
Study Lists

COMPLETION STANDARDS:

- Demonstrate understanding during oral quizzing by instructor at completion of lesson.
- Student completes Chapter 6 questions for Sections A, B, and C with a minimum passing score of 80%. Instructor reviews incorrect responses to ensure complete student understanding prior to progression to Ground Lesson 8.

STAGE II
GROUND LESSON 8

LESSON REFERENCES:

FAR/AIM —
Private Pilot FARs

FAR/AIM CD-ROM —
PRIVATE PILOT FARS

RECOMMENDED SEQUENCE:
1. Lesson Introduction
2. Class Discussion

LESSON OBJECTIVES:
- Understand the appropriate Federal Aviation Regulations in the Private Pilot Recommended Study List.
- Gain specific knowledge of those FARs which govern student solo flight operations, private pilot privileges, limitations, and National Tansportation Safety Board (NTSB) accident reporting requirements.

ACADEMIC CONTENT:
❏ FAR Part 1
❏ FAR Part 61
❏ FAR Part 91
❏ NTSB 830

STUDY ASSIGNMENT:

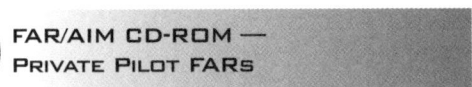

PRIVATE PILOT MANUAL —
Chapter 7, Interpreting Weather Data

COMPLETION STANDARDS:
- Demonstrate understanding during oral quizzing by instructor at completion of lesson.
- Student completes Ground Lesson 8 Private Pilot FAR Exercises with a minimum passing score of 80%. Instructor reviews incorrect responses to ensure complete student understanding prior to progressing to Ground Lesson 9.

STAGE II
GROUND LESSON 9

LESSON REFERENCES:

 PRIVATE PILOT MANUAL —
Chapter 7, Interpreting Weather Data

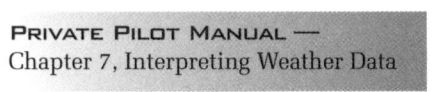 PART III, CHAPTER 7

RECOMMENDED SEQUENCE:
1. Lesson Introduction and Video Presentation
2. Class Discussion

LESSON OBJECTIVES:
- Learn how to obtain and interpret weather reports, formats, and graphic charts.
- Become familiar with the sources of weather information during preflight planning and while in flight.
- Recognize critical weather situations described by weather reports and forecasts.

ACADEMIC CONTENT:
SECTION A — THE FORECASTING PROCESS
❏ Forecasting Methods
❏ Types of Forecasts
❏ Compiling and Processing Weather Data
❏ Forecasting Accuracy and Limitations

SECTION B — PRINTED REPORTS AND FORECASTS
❏ Aviation Routine Weather Report (METAR)
❏ Radar Weather Reports
❏ Pilot Weather Reports
❏ Terminal Aerodrome Forecast (TAF)
❏ Aviation Area Forecast
❏ Winds and Temperatures Aloft Forecast
❏ Severe Weather Reports and Forecasts
❏ AIRMET/SIGMET/Convective SIGMET

SECTION C — GRAPHIC WEATHER PRODUCTS
❏ Surface Analysis Chart
❏ Weather Depiction Chart

- ☐ Radar Summary Chart
- ☐ Satellite Weather Pictures
- ☐ Low-Level Significant Weather Prog
- ☐ Severe Weather Outlook Chart
- ☐ Forecast Winds and Temperatures Aloft Chart
- ☐ Volcanic Ash Forecast and Dispersion Chart

SECTION D — SOURCES OF WEATHER INFORMATION

- ☐ Preflight Weather Sources
- ☐ In-Flight Weather Sources
- ☐ Enroute Flight Advisory Service
- ☐ Weather Radar Services
- ☐ Automated Weather Reporting Systems

STUDY ASSIGNMENT:

PRIVATE PILOT MANUAL —
Review Chapters 6 and 7, and the *FAR/AIM*
in preparation for the Stage II Exam.

COMPLETION STANDARDS:

- Demonstrate understanding during oral quizzing by instructor at completion of lesson.
- Student completes Chapter 7 questions for Sections A, B, C, and D with a minimum passing score of 80%. Instructor reviews incorrect responses to ensure complete student understanding prior to progressing to the Stage II Exam.

STAGE II
GROUND LESSON 10
STAGE II EXAM

LESSON REFERENCES:

PRIVATE PILOT MANUAL —
Chapters 6 and 7
FAR/AIM — Private Pilot FARs

PART III, CHAPTERS 6 AND 7

RECOMMENDED SEQUENCE:
1. Lesson Introduction
2. Testing
3. Critique

LESSON OBJECTIVES:
- Demonstrate comprehension of the material presented in Chapters 6 and 7 of the *Private Pilot Manual* and the FARs that apply to private pilot operations, including private pilot privileges, limitations, and NTSB accident reporting requirements.

ACADEMIC CONTENT:
STAGE II EXAM
❏ Meteorology for Pilots
❏ Federal Aviation Regulations
❏ Interpreting Weather Data

STUDY ASSIGNMENT:

PRIVATE PILOT MANUAL —
Chapter 8, Airplane Performance

COMPLETION STANDARDS:

This lesson and stage are complete when the student has completed the Stage II Exam with a minimum passing score of 80%, and the instructor has reviewed each incorrect response to ensure complete understanding before the student progresses to Stage III.

STAGE III

STAGE OBJECTIVES

During this stage, the student will learn how to predict performance and control the weight and balance condition of the airplane. In addition, the student will be introduced to pilotage, dead reckoning, and navigation equipment. This includes understanding the basic concepts of how to use aeronautical charts, plotters, flight computers, and flight publications to plan cross-country flight. The student also will learn how to use VOR, ADF, and advanced navigation systems. In addition, the student will obtain an understanding of the physiological factors which can affect both pilot and passengers during flight. Finally, the student will learn how to conduct comprehensive preflight planning for cross-country flights and gain insight into factors affecting aeronautical decision making.

STAGE COMPLETION STANDARDS

This stage is complete when the student has completed the Stage III written exam with a minimum passing score of 80%, and the instructor has reviewed each incorrect response to ensure complete understanding.

STAGE III
GROUND LESSON 11

LESSON REFERENCES:

 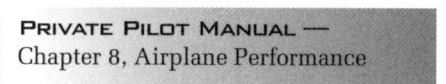
PRIVATE PILOT MANUAL —
Chapter 8, Airplane Performance

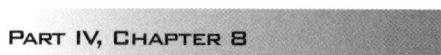
PART IV, CHAPTER 8

RECOMMENDED SEQUENCE:
1. Lesson Introduction and Video Presentation
2. Class Discussion

LESSON OBJECTIVES:
- Learn how to use data supplied by the manufacturer to predict airplane performance, including takeoff and landing distances and fuel requirements.
- Learn to compute and control the weight and balance condition of a typical training airplane.
- Become familiar with basic functions of aviation computers.
- Understand the effects of density altitude on takeoff and climb performance.

ACADEMIC CONTENT:
SECTION A — PREDICTING PERFORMANCE
❑ Aircraft Performance and Design
❑ Chart Presentations
❑ Factors Affecting Performance
❑ Takeoff and Landing Performance
❑ Climb Performance
❑ Cruise Performance
❑ Using Performance Charts

SECTION B — WEIGHT AND BALANCE
❑ Importance of Weight
❑ Importance of Balance
❑ Terminology
❑ Principles of Weight and Balance
❑ Computation Method
❑ Table Method
❑ Graph Method

❏ Weight-Shift Formula
❏ Effects of Operating at High Total Weights
❏ Flight at Various CG Positions

SECTION C — FLIGHT COMPUTERS

❏ Mechanical Flight Computers
❏ Time, Speed, and Distance
❏ Airspeed and Density Altitude Computations
❏ Wind Problems
❏ Conversions
❏ Multi-Part Problems
❏ Electronic Flight Computers
❏ Modes and Basic Operations

STUDY ASSIGNMENT:

PRIVATE PILOT MANUAL —
Chapter 9, Navigation

COMPLETION STANDARDS:

• Demonstrate understanding during oral quizzing by instructor at completion of lesson.
• Student completes Chapter 8 questions for Sections A, B, and C with a minimum passing score of 80%. Instructor reviews incorrect responses to ensure complete student understanding prior to progressing to Ground Lesson 12.

STAGE III
GROUND LESSON 12

LESSON REFERENCES:

PRIVATE PILOT MANUAL —
Chapter 9, Navigation

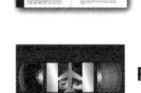

PART IV, CHAPTER 9

RECOMMENDED SEQUENCE:
1. Lesson Introduction and Video Presentation
2. Class Discussion
3. PCATD

LESSON OBJECTIVES:
- Learn the basic concepts for VFR navigation using pilotage, dead reckoning, and aircraft navigation systems.
- Become familiar with guidelines and recommended procedures related to flight planning, use of an FAA Flight Plan, VFR cruising altitudes, and lost procedures.
- Gain a basic understanding of VFR navigation using pilotage, dead reckoning, and navigation systems.

ACADEMIC CONTENT:
SECTION A — PILOTAGE AND DEAD RECKONING
❑ Pilotage
❑ Dead Reckoning
❑ Flight Planning
❑ VFR Cruising Altitudes
❑ Flight Plan
❑ Lost Procedures

SECTION B — VOR NAVIGATION
❑ VOR Operations
❑ Ground and Airborne Equipment
❑ Basic Procedures
❑ VOR Orientation and Navigation

❏ VOR Checkpoints and Test Signals
❏ VOR Precautions
❏ Horizontal Situation Indicator
❏ Distance Measuring Equipment (DME)

SECTION C — ADF NAVIGATION
❏ ADF Equipment
❏ Orientation
❏ Homing
❏ ADF Intercepts and Tracking
❏ Movable-Card Indicators
❏ Radio Magnetic Indicator
❏ ADF Precautions

SECTION D — ADVANCED NAVIGATION
❏ VORTAC-Based Area Navigation
❏ Long Range Navigation (LORAN)
❏ Inertial Navigation System
❏ Global Positioning System

STUDY ASSIGNMENT:

PRIVATE PILOT MANUAL —
Chapter 10, Applying Human Factors
Principles

COMPLETION STANDARDS:

• Demonstrate under-standing during oral quizzing by instructor at completion of lesson.

• Student completes Chapter 9 questions for Sections A, B, C, and D with a minimum pass-ing score of 80%. Instructor reviews incorrect responses to ensure complete stu-dent understanding prior to progressing to Ground Lesson 13.

STAGE III
GROUND LESSON 13

LESSON REFERENCES:

PRIVATE PILOT MANUAL —
Chapter 10, Applying Human Factors Principles

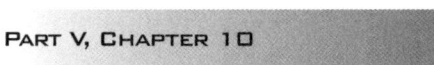

PART V, CHAPTER 10

RECOMMENDED SEQUENCE:
1. Lesson Introduction and Video Presentation
2. Class Discussion

LESSON OBJECTIVES:
- Gain an insight into important aviation physiological factors as they relate to private pilot operations.
- Become familiar with the accepted procedures and concepts pertaining to aeronautical decision making and judgment, including cockpit resource management and human factors training.
- Gain a basic understanding of aeronautical decision making and judgment.

ACADEMIC CONTENT:
SECTION A — AVIATION PHYSIOLOGY
❑ Vision in Flight
❑ Night Vision
❑ Visual Illusions
❑ Disorientation
❑ Respiration
❑ Hypoxia
❑ Hyperventilation

SECTION B — AERONAUTICAL DECISION MAKING
❑ Applying the Decision Making Process
❑ Pilot-in-Command Responsibility
❑ Communication
❑ Workload Management
❑ Situational Awareness
❑ Resource Use
❑ Applying Human Factors Training

STUDY ASSIGNMENT:

PRIVATE PILOT MANUAL —
Chapter 11, Flying Cross-Country

COMPLETION STANDARDS:

- Demonstrate under-standing during oral quizzing by instructor at completion of lesson.
- Student completes Chapter 10 questions for Sections A, and B with a minimum pass-ing score of 80%. Instructor reviews incorrect responses to ensure complete stu-dent understanding prior to progressing to Ground Lesson 14.

STAGE III
GROUND LESSON 14

LESSON REFERENCES:

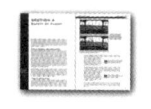  **PRIVATE PILOT MANUAL —**
Chapter 11, Flying Cross-Country

RECOMMENDED SEQUENCE:
1. Lesson Introduction and Video Presentation
2. Class Discussion
3. PCATD

LESSON OBJECTIVES:
• Develop a sound understanding of the planning process for a cross-country flight.
• Become familiar with the details of flying a typical cross-country flight, including evaluation of in-flight weather and decisions for alternative actions, such as a diversion.
• Understand how to plan for alternatives.

ACADEMIC CONTENT:
SECTION A — THE FLIGHT PLANNING PROCESS
❏ Developing the Route
❏ Preflight Weather Briefing
❏ Completing the Navigation Log
❏ Flight Plan
❏ Preflight Inspection

SECTION B — THE FLIGHT
❏ Departure
❏ Centennial Airport to Pueblo Memorial Airport
❏ Pueblo Memorial Airport to La Junta Municipal Airport
❏ La Junta Municipal Airport to Centennial Airport
❏ Diversion to Limon Municipal Airport
❏ Return to Centennial Airport

STUDY ASSIGNMENT:

PRIVATE PILOT MANUAL —
Chapters 8–11 in preparation for the
Stage III Exam

**COMPLETION
STANDARDS:**

- Demonstrate under-
standing during oral
quizzing by instructor
at completion of lesson.
- Student completes
Chapter 11 questions
for Sections A, and B
with a minimum pass-
ing score of 80%.
Instructor reviews
incorrect responses to
ensure complete stu-
dent understanding
prior to progressing to
the Stage III Exam.

STAGE III
GROUND LESSON 15
STAGE III EXAM

LESSON REFERENCES:

 PRIVATE PILOT MANUAL —
Chapters 8–11

 PARTS IV AND V, CHAPTERS 8–10   ←

RECOMMENDED SEQUENCE:
1. Lesson Introduction
2. Testing
3. Critique

LESSON OBJECTIVES:
- Demonstrate comprehension of the material presented in Chapters 8 through 11 of the *Private Pilot Manual.*

ACADEMIC CONTENT:
STAGE III EXAM
- ❏ Airplane Performance
- ❏ Navigation
- ❏ Human Factors Principles
- ❏ Aeronautical Decision Making
- ❏ Flying Cross-Country

STUDY ASSIGNMENT:

 PRIVATE PILOT MANUAL —
Review the entire manual, as necessary, in preparation for
Private Pilot Final Exam "A."

**COMPLETION
STANDARDS:**

This lesson and stage are
complete when the stu-
dent has completed the
Stage III Exam with a minimum passing score of
80%, and the instructor
has reviewed each incor-
rect response to ensure
complete understanding
before the student pro-
gresses to the course final
examinations.

STAGE III
GROUND LESSON 16
FINAL EXAM "A"

LESSON REFERENCES:

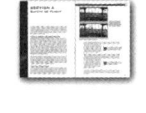

PRIVATE PILOT MANUAL —
Chapters 1–11

PARTS I–V, CHAPTERS 2–10   ←

RECOMMENDED SEQUENCE:
1. Lesson Introduction
2. Testing
3. Critique

LESSON OBJECTIVES:
- Demonstrate comprehension of the material presented in this course in preparation for the FAA Private Pilot Airmen Knowledge Test.

ACADEMIC CONTENT:
❏ Private Pilot Final Exam "A"

STUDY ASSIGNMENT:

Review any deficient subject areas based on the results of Final Exam "A." Review in preparation for Final Exam "B."

COMPLETION STANDARDS:

Each student must complete the Private Pilot Final Exam "A" with a minimum passing score of 80%, and the instructor should review each incorrect response to ensure complete understanding before the student progresses to the Private Pilot Final Exam "B."

STAGE III
GROUND LESSON 17
FINAL EXAM "B"

LESSON REFERENCES:

PRIVATE PILOT MANUAL —
Chapters 1–11

PARTS I–V, CHAPTERS 2–10   ←

RECOMMENDED SEQUENCE:
1. Lesson Introduction
2. Testing
3. Critique

LESSON OBJECTIVES:
- Demonstrate comprehension of the academic material presented in this course and the student's readiness to complete the FAA Private Pilot Airmen Knowledge Test.

ACADEMIC CONTENT:
❑ Private Pilot Final Exam "B"

STUDY ASSIGNMENT:

Review any deficient subject areas based on the results of Final Exam "B." Review in preparation for the FAA Private Pilot Airmen Knowledge Test.

COMPLETION STANDARDS:

Each student must complete Private Pilot Final Exam "B" with a minimum passing score of 80%, and the instructor should review each incorrect response to ensure complete student understanding.

PRIVATE PILOT FLIGHT TRAINING SYLLABUS

FLIGHT TRAINING COURSE OBJECTIVES

The student will obtain the necessary aeronautical skill and experience necessary to meet the requirements for a private pilot certificate with an airplane category rating and single-engine land class rating.

FLIGHT TRAINING COURSE COMPLETION REQUIREMENTS

The student must demonstrate through flight tests and school records that the necessary aeronautical skill and experience requirements to obtain a private pilot certificate with an airplane category rating and single-engine land class rating have been met.

STAGE I

STAGE OBJECTIVES

During this stage, the student obtains the foundation for all future aviation training. The student becomes familiar with the training airplane and learns how the airplane controls are used to establish and maintain specific flight attitudes and ground tracks. The student also will gain the proficiency to solo the training airplane in the traffic pattern.

STAGE COMPLETION STANDARDS

At the completion of this stage, the student will demonstrate proficiency in basic flight maneuvers, and will have successfully soloed in the traffic pattern. In addition, the student will have the proficiency required for introduction of maximum performance takeoff and landing procedures in Stage II.

STAGE II

STAGE OBJECTIVES

This stage allows the student to expand the skills learned in the previous stage. The student is introduced to short-field and soft-field takeoff and landing procedures, as well as night flying, which are important steps in preparation for cross-country training. Additionally, greater emphasis is placed on attitude control by instrument reference to increase the student's overall competence. In the cross-country phase, the student will learn to plan and conduct cross-country flights using pilotage, dead reckoning, and radio navigation systems, and how to safely conduct flights in the National Airspace System.

STAGE COMPLETION STANDARDS

This stage is complete when the student can accurately plan and conduct cross-country flights. In addition, the student will have the proficiency to safely demonstrate consistent results in performing short-field and soft-field takeoffs and landings and night operations. The proficiency level must be such that the successful and safe outcome of each task is never seriously in doubt.

STAGE III

STAGE OBJECTIVES

During this stage, the student will gain additional proficiency in solo cross-country operations and will receive instructions in preparation for the end-of-course stage check.

STAGE COMPLETION STANDARDS

This stage will be complete when the student demonstrates performance of private pilot operations at a standard that meets or exceeds the minimum performance criteria established in the practical test standards for a private pilot certificate.

STAGE I
FLIGHT LESSON 1
DUAL — LOCAL (0.5)

LESSON OBJECTIVES:

- Become familiar with the training airplane and its systems.
- Learn about certificates, documents, and checklists. Understand how to conduct the necessary preflight activities.Learn about the functions of the flight controls, and how they are used to maintain specific attitudes.
- Gain an understanding of preflight preparation and procedures.

PREFLIGHT DISCUSSION:

- ❏ Fitness for flight
- ❏ Positive Exchange of Flight Controls
- ❏ Certificates and documents
- ❏ Airplane logbooks
- ❏ Airplane servicing
- ❏ Fuel grades

INTRODUCE:

- ❏ Use of Checklists
- ❏ Preflight Inspection
- ❏ Certificates and Documents
- ❏ Airplane Servicing
- ❏ Operation of Systems
- ❏ Equipment Checks
- ❏ Location of First Aid Kit
- ❏ Location of Fire Extinguisher
- ❏ Engine Starting
- ❏ Radio Communications
- ❏ Taxiing
- ❏ Before Takeoff Check
- ❏ Normal Takeoff and Climb
- ❏ Straight-and-Level Flight
- ❏ Climbs, Descents, and Level Offs
- ❏ Medium Banked Turns in Both Directions
- ❏ Normal Approach and Landing
- ❏ After Landing Procedures
- ❏ Parking and Securing the Airplane

STUDY ASSIGNMENT:

PRIVATE PILOT MANEUVERS —
Ground Operations and
Basic Maneuvers

MANEUVERS MULTIMEDIA TRAINING —
Ground Operations and Basic Maneuvers

COMPLETION
STANDARDS:

- Display basic knowledge of aircraft systems and the necessity of checking their operation before flight.
- Become familiar with the control systems and how they are used to maneuver the airplane on the ground and in the air.

STAGE I
FLIGHT LESSON 2
DUAL — LOCAL (1.0)

LESSON REFERENCES

 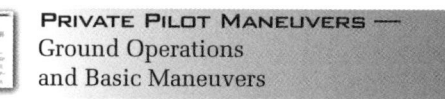
PRIVATE PILOT MANEUVERS —
Ground Operations
and Basic Maneuvers

MANEUVERS MULTIMEDIA TRAINING —
Ground Operations and Basic Maneuvers

 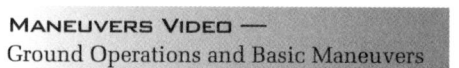
MANEUVERS VIDEO —
Ground Operations and Basic Maneuvers

LESSON OBJECTIVES:

• Review procedures and maneuvers introduced in Flight Lesson 1, especially pre-flight activities, ground operations, and attitude control during basic maneuvers using visual reference (VR).

• Introduce additional procedures and maneuvers.

• Emphasis will be on correct procedures for preflight and ground operations.

PREFLIGHT DISCUSSION:

❏ Human factors concepts
❏ Preflight activities
❏ Minimum equipment list concept
❏ Engine starting
❏ Airport and runway markings and lighting
❏ Ground operations, including crosswind taxiing
❏ Collision avoidance precautions
❏ Airspeed and configuration changes

INTRODUCE:

❏ Minimum Equipment List
❏ Airport and Runway Markings and Lighting
❏ Crosswind Taxi

❏ Airspeed and Configuration Changes
❏ Flight at Approach Airspeed
❏ Traffic Patterns
❏ Descents in High and Low Drag Configurations

REVIEW:
❏ Preflight Inspection
❏ Certificates and Documents
❏ Operation of Systems
❏ Positive Exchange of Flight Controls
❏ Use of Checklists
❏ Engine Starting
❏ Radio Communications
❏ Taxiing
❏ Before Takeoff Check
❏ Normal Takeoff and Climb
❏ Straight-and-Level Flight (VR)
❏ Climbs (VR)
❏ Descents (VR)
❏ Medium Banked Turns in Both Directions (VR)
❏ Normal Approach and Landing
❏ After Landing Procedures
❏ Parking and Securing the Airplane
❏ Airplane Servicing

POSTFLIGHT DISCUSSION AND PREVIEW OF NEXT LESSON

STUDY ASSIGNMENT:

PRIVATE PILOT MANEUVERS —
Flight Maneuvers

MANEUVERS MULTIMEDIA TRAINING —
Flight Maneuvers

COMPLETION STANDARDS:

• Display increased proficiency in preflight activities, ground operations, and coordinated airplane attitude control.

• Perform takeoffs with instructor assistance.

• Be familiar with control usage necessary to maintain altitude within ± 250 feet during airspeed and configuration changes.

• Exhibit understanding of attitude control by visual reference (VR).

STAGE I
FLIGHT LESSON 3
DUAL — LOCAL (1.0)

Note: A view-limiting device is required for the .2 hours of dual instrument time allocated to Flight Lesson 3.

LESSON REFERENCES

PRIVATE PILOT MANEUVERS —
Flight Maneuvers

MANEUVERS MULTIMEDIA TRAINING —
Flight Maneuvers

MANEUVERS VIDEO —
Flight Maneuvers

LESSON OBJECTIVES:

- Review airspeed control during basic maneuvers and traffic pattern operations.
- Introduce stalls from various flight attitudes to increase understanding of airplane control during normal and critical flight conditions.
- Introduce attitude control by instrument reference (IR).
- Emphasis will be directed to proper execution of the listed basic maneuvers and procedures, particularly takeoffs, traffic patterns, and landings.

PREFLIGHT DISCUSSION:

❏ Situational awareness
❏ Basic instrument maneuvers
❏ Preflight planning, operation of powerplant, aircraft systems, and engine runup procedures
❏ Visual scanning and collision avoidance precautions
❏ Windshear and wake turbulence avoidance procedures

INTRODUCE:

❏ Flight at Various Airspeeds From Cruise to Slow Flight
❏ Maneuvering During Slow Flight
❏ Power-Off Stalls
❏ Power-On Stalls

- ❑ Straight-and-Level Flight (IR)
- ❑ Constant Airspeed Climbs (IR)
- ❑ Constant Airspeed Descents (IR)

REVIEW:
- ❑ Use of Checklists
- ❑ Airplane Servicing
- ❑ Preflight Inspection
- ❑ Minimum Equipment List
- ❑ Engine Starting
- ❑ Radio Communications
- ❑ Before Takeoff Check
- ❑ Normal Takeoff and Climb
- ❑ Traffic Patterns
- ❑ Collision Avoidance Precautions
- ❑ Airspeed and Configuration Changes
- ❑ Descents in High and Low Drag Configurations
- ❑ Flight at Approach Airspeed
- ❑ Normal Approach and Landing
- ❑ Airport and Runway Markings and Lighting
- ❑ Parking and Securing the Airplane

POSTFLIGHT DISCUSSION AND PREVIEW OF NEXT LESSON

STUDY ASSIGNMENT:

PRIVATE PILOT MANEUVERS —
Flight Maneuvers and Emergency Landing Procedures

MANEUVERS MULTIMEDIA TRAINING —
Flight Maneuvers and Emergency Landing Procedures

COMPLETION STANDARDS:
- Display increased proficiency in coordinated airplane attitude control during basic maneuvers.
- Perform unassisted takeoffs.
- Demonstrate correct communications and traffic pattern procedures.
- Landings completed with instructor assistance.
- Maintain altitude within ± 250 feet during airspeed transitions and while maneuvering at slow airspeeds.
- Indicate basic ability to control attitude by instrument reference (IR).

STAGE I
FLIGHT LESSON 4
DUAL — LOCAL (1.0)

Note: A view-limiting device is required for the .2 hours of dual instrument time allocated to Flight Lesson 4.

LESSON REFERENCES

PRIVATE PILOT MANEUVERS —
Flight Maneuvers and Emergency
Landing Procedures

MANEUVERS MULTIMEDIA TRAINING —
Flight Maneuvers and Emergency
Landing Procedures

MANEUVERS VIDEO —
Flight Maneuvers and Emergency
Landing Procedures

LESSON OBJECTIVES:

- Practice the maneuvers listed for review to gain additional proficiency and demonstrate the ability to recognize and recover from stalls.
- The student will also receive instruction and practice in the maneuvers and procedures listed for introduction, including emergency operations and additional practice of airplane control by instrument reference (IR).
- Instructor may demonstrate secondary, accelerated maneuver, crossed-controlled, and elevator trim stalls.
- Emphasis will be on procedures related to airport operations, steep turns, slow flight, stalls, and stall recovery.

PREFLIGHT DISCUSSION:
❑ Wake turbulence avoidance
❑ Workload management
❑ Pilot-in-command responsibilities
❑ Emergency procedures and equipment malfunctions
❑ Emergency field selection

INTRODUCE:
❑ Systems and Equipment Malfunctions
❑ Emergency Procedures
❑ Emergency Descent
❑ Emergency Approach and Landing

- Emergency Equipment and Survival Gear
- ❏ Climbing and Descending Turns (VR) (IR)
- ❏ Steep Turns
- ❏ Turns to Headings (VR) (IR)
- ❏ Flight at Slow Airspeeds with Realistic Distractions, and the Recognition and Recovery from Stalls Entered from Straight Flight and from Turns
- ❏ Spin Awareness
- ❏ Demonstrated Stalls (Secondary, Accelerated Maneuver, Crossed-Control, and Elevator Trim)

NOTE: *The demonstrated stalls are not a proficiency requirement for private pilot certification. The purpose of the demonstrations is to help the student learn how to recognize, prevent, and if necessary, recover before the stall develops into a spin. These stalls should not be practiced without a qualified flight instructor. In addition, some stalls may be prohibited in some airplanes.*

REVIEW:
- ❏ Airport and Runway Markings and Lighting
- ❏ Airspeed and Configuration Changes
- ❏ Flight at Approach Speed
- ❏ Flight at Various Airspeeds From Cruise to Slow Flight
- ❏ Maneuvering During Slow Flight
- ❏ Power-Off Stalls
- ❏ Power-On Stalls
- ❏ Normal Takeoffs and Landings
- ❏ Collision Avoidance Precautions
- ❏ Traffic Patterns

POSTFLIGHT DISCUSSION AND PREVIEW OF NEXT LESSON

STUDY ASSIGNMENT:

PRIVATE PILOT MANEUVERS —
Ground Reference Maneuvers

MANEUVERS MULTIMEDIA TRAINING —
Ground Reference Maneuvers

NOTE: *All preflight duties and procedures will be performed and evaluated prior to each flight. Therefore, they will not appear in the content outlines.*

COMPLETION STANDARDS:
- Display increased proficiency in coordinated airplane attitude control during basic maneuvers.
- Perform unassisted takeoffs.
- Demonstrate correct communications and traffic pattern procedures.
- Landings completed with instructor assistance.
- Demonstrate basic understanding of steep turns, slow flight, stalls, stall recovery, and emergency operations.
- Complete demonstrated stalls
- Indicate basic understanding of airplane control by use of the flight instruments.

STAGE I
FLIGHT LESSON 5
DUAL — LOCAL (1.0)

Note: A view-limiting device is required for the .2 hours of dual instrument time allocated to Flight Lesson 5.

LESSON REFERENCES

PRIVATE PILOT MANEUVERS —
Ground Reference Maneuvers

MANEUVERS MULTIMEDIA TRAINING —
Ground Reference Maneuvers

MANEUVERS VIDEO —
Ground Reference Maneuvers

LESSON OBJECTIVES:

- Practice the review maneuvers to gain proficiency.
- Introduce ground reference maneuvers and maneuvering at slow airspeeds by instrument reference.
- Emphasis will be on emergency landing procedures.

PREFLIGHT DISCUSSION:

❏ Situational awareness
❏ Realistic distractions
❏ Determining wind direction

INTRODUCE:

❏ Rectangular Courses
❏ S-Turns
❏ Turns Around a Point
❏ Maneuvering During Slow Flight (IR)

REVIEW:

❏ Positive Exchange of Flight Controls
❏ Maneuvering During Slow Flight (VR)
❏ Power-Off Stalls

- ❏ Power-On Stalls
- ❏ Flight at Slow Airspeeds with Realistic Distractions, and the Recognition and Recovery from Stalls Entered from Straight Flight and from Turns
- ❏ Spin Awareness
- ❏ Emergency Descent
- ❏ Emergency Approach and Landing
- ❏ Emergency Equipment and Survival Gear
- ❏ Normal Takeoffs and Landings
- ❏ Turns to Headings (VR)
- ❏ Turns to Headings (IR)

POSTFLIGHT DISCUSSION AND PREVIEW OF NEXT LESSON

STUDY ASSIGNMENT:

PRIVATE PILOT MANEUVERS —
Airport Operations

MANEUVERS MULTIMEDIA TRAINING —
Airport Operations

COMPLETION STANDARDS:

- Display increased proficiency in coordinated airplane attitude control during basic maneuvers.
- Perform unassisted takeoffs.
- Demonstrate correct communications and traffic pattern procedures.
- Landings completed with a minimum of instructor assistance.
- Maintain altitude ± 225 feet and headings ± 15° during straight-and-level flight.
- Demonstrate the ability to recognize and recover from stalls.
- Indicate basic understanding of attitude instrument flying and emergency landing procedures.

STAGE I
FLIGHT LESSON 6
DUAL — LOCAL (1.0)

LESSON REFERENCE

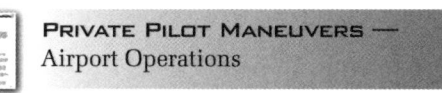

PRIVATE PILOT MANEUVERS —
Airport Operations

MANEUVERS MULTIMEDIA TRAINING —
Airport Operations

MANEUVERS VIDEO —
Airport Operations

LESSON OBJECTIVES:

- Practice the review maneuvers to gain proficiency.
- Introduce go-arounds, slips, and crosswind takeoffs and landings so the student may begin to learn the procedures during varying wind conditions.
- Review ground reference maneuvers.
- Emphasis will be on go-arounds and any of the more advanced maneuvers that appear to be difficult for the student.

PREFLIGHT DISCUSSION:

❏ Communication
❏ Workload management
❏ Lost communication procedures
❏ Runway incursion avoidance
❏ Land and Hold Short Operations (LAHSO)

INTRODUCE:

❏ Go-arounds From a Rejected Landing
❏ Forward Slips to Landing
❏ Crosswind Takeoff and Climb
❏ Crosswind Approach and Landing
❏ ATC Light Signals
❏ Runway Incursion Avoidance
❏ Land and Hold Short Operations (LAHSO)

REVIEW:

❏ Rectangular Courses
❏ S-Turns

- ❏ Turns Around a Point
- ❏ Normal Takeoffs and Landings
- ❏ Traffic Patterns
- ❏ Wake Turbulence Avoidance
- ❏ Emergency Descent
- ❏ Emergency Approach and Landing

POSTFLIGHT DISCUSSION AND PREVIEW OF NEXT LESSON

STUDY ASSIGNMENT:

PRIVATE PILOT MANEUVERS —
References for Flight Lessons 1-6

MANEUVERS MULTIMEDIA TRAINING —
References for Flight Lessons 1-6

COMPLETION STANDARDS:

- Display increased proficiency in coordinated airplane attitude control.
- Demonstrate ability to fly a specific ground track while maintaining altitude ± 200 feet.
- Demonstrate basic understanding of how the forward slip is used for an approach to a landing.
- Indicate knowledge of crosswind takeoff/ landing procedures and go-arounds.

NOTE: *Student pilots conducting solo flight operations are not authorized to participate in LAHSO.*

STAGE I
FLIGHT LESSON 7
DUAL — LOCAL (1.0)

Note: A view-limiting device is required for the .2 hours of dual instrument time allocated to Flight Lesson 7

LESSON REFERENCE

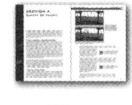

PRIVATE PILOT MANEUVERS —
References for Flight Lessons 1-6

MANEUVERS MULTIMEDIA TRAINING —
References for Flight Lessons 1-6

MANEUVERS VIDEO —
References for Flight Lessons 1-6

LESSON OBJECTIVES:
- Practice instrument flight maneuvers, takeoffs, landings, and emergency procedures in preparation for solo flight.
- Review those maneuvers and procedures that appear to be difficult for the student.
- Emphasis on ground reference maneuvers and emergency operations.

PREFLIGHT DISCUSSION:
❏ Sections of FAR Parts 61 and 91 applicable to private pilots
❏ Airspace rules and procedures for the airport where solo flight will be performed
❏ Flight characteristics and operational limitations for the make and model of aircraft to be flown in solo flight

REVIEW:
❏ Straight-and-Level Flight (VR-IR)
❏ Steep Turns
❏ Constant Airspeed Climbs (VR-IR)
❏ Constant Airspeed Descents (VR-IR)
❏ Climbing and Descending Turns
❏ Turns to Headings (IR)
❏ Rectangular Courses
❏ S-Turns

❏ Crosswind Takeoff and Climb
❏ Crosswind Approach and Landing
❏ Runway Incursion Avoidance
❏ Land and Hold Short Operations (LAHSO)   ⟵
❏ Go-Around From a Rejected Landing
❏ Forward Slips to Landing
❏ Systems and Equipment Malfunctions
❏ Emergency Procedures
❏ Emergency Descent
❏ Emergency Approach and Landing
❏ ATC Light Signals

POSTFLIGHT DISCUSSION AND PREVIEW OF NEXT LESSON

STUDY ASSIGNMENT:

Prepare for the Presolo Written Exam and Briefing. The student will be provided with the exam questions in advance.

COMPLETION STANDARDS:

- Display increased proficiency and skill in instrument scan and interpretation during practice of instrument flight maneuvers.
- Takeoffs, landings, and go-arounds should be performed without instructor assistance.
- Emergency procedures should be accomplished with minimal assistance.
- Ground reference maneuvers should indicate increasing proficiency and precision.

STAGE I
FLIGHT LESSON 8
DUAL — LOCAL (1.0)

Note: A view-limiting device is required for the .2 hours of dual instrument time allocated to Flight Lesson 8.

LESSON OBJECTIVES:

• Prior to this flight, the instructor will administer and grade the Presolo Written Exam and Briefing.

• Practice the listed review maneuvers and/or procedures, including emergency operations and basic instrument maneuvers, to help the student gain proficiency and confidence.

• Emphasis will be directed toward correction of any faulty tendencies to prepare the student for the first solo.

PREFLIGHT DISCUSSION:

❏ Presolo Written Exam critique
❏ Presolo flight training requirements

REVIEW:

❏ Operation of Systems
❏ Preflight Inspection
❏ Engine Starting
❏ Radio Communication
❏ Normal and/or Crosswind Taxiing
❏ Before Takeoff Check
❏ Normal and/or Crosswind Takeoff
❏ Climbing and Descending Turns
❏ Collision Avoidance Precautions
❏ Wake Turbulence Avoidance
❏ Straight-and-Level Flight (IR)
❏ Turns to Headings (IR)
❏ Maneuvering During Slow Flight (IR)
❏ Power-Off Stalls
❏ Power-On Stalls
❏ Maneuvering During Slow Flight
❏ Flight at Slow Airspeeds with Realistic Distractions, and the Recognition and Recovery from Stalls Entered from Straight Flight and from Turns
❏ Spin Awareness

❏ Rectangular Courses
❏ S-Turns
❏ Turns Around a Point
❏ Systems and Equipment Malfunctions
❏ Emergency Procedures
❏ Emergency Descent
❏ Emergency Approach and Landing
❏ Traffic Patterns
❏ Forward Slips to Landing
❏ Go-Around From a Rejected Landing
❏ Normal and/or Crosswind Approach and Landing

POSTFLIGHT DISCUSSION AND PREVIEW OF NEXT LESSON

STUDY ASSIGNMENT:

Review any deficient subject areas based on the results of the Presolo Written Exam. Review *Private Pilot Maneuvers* and *Maneuvers Multimedia Training* as required, or as assigned by the instructor.

COMPLETION STANDARDS:

- This lesson is complete when the student successfully passes the Presolo Written Exam with a minimum score of 80%, and the instructor has reviewed each incorrect response to ensure complete student understanding.
- Demonstrate the ability and readiness for supervised solo flight in the traffic pattern.
- Exhibit understanding of attitude instrument flying.
- Indicate good understanding of local airport and airspace rules as well as systems and equipment malfunctions and related emergency procedures.

STAGE I
FLIGHT LESSON 9
DUAL — LOCAL (0.5)
SOLO — LOCAL (0.5)

LESSON OBJECTIVES:

- During the dual portion of the lesson, the instructor will review takeoff and landing procedures to check the student's readiness for solo flight.
- In the second portion of the lesson, the student will fly the first supervised solo flight in the local traffic pattern.
- Emphasis will be on the correct procedures and techniques for the student's first solo.

PREFLIGHT DISCUSSION:
❏ Any student questions
❏ Student pilot supervised solo flight operations in the local traffic pattern

REVIEW:
❏ Engine Starting
❏ Radio Communications
❏ Normal and/or Crosswind Taxiing
❏ Before Takeoff Check
❏ Normal Takeoffs
❏ Traffic Patterns
❏ Go-Around From a Rejected Landing
❏ Normal Landings

INTRODUCE:

SUPERVISED SOLO
❏ Radio Communications
❏ Taxiing
❏ Before Takeoff Check
❏ Normal Takeoffs and Climbs (3)
❏ Traffic Patterns
❏ Normal Approaches and Landings (3)
❏ After Landing Procedures
❏ Parking and Securing

POSTFLIGHT DISCUSSION AND PREVIEW OF NEXT LESSON

STUDY ASSIGNMENT:

Review, as required, in preparation for the Stage I Check in Flight Lesson 10.

COMPLETION STANDARDS:

- The student will display the ability to solo the training airplane safely in the traffic pattern. At no time will the safety of the flight be in question.
- Complete solo flight in the local traffic pattern as directed by the instructor.

STAGE I
FLIGHT LESSON 10
Dual — Local (1.0)
Stage Check

LESSON OBJECTIVES:

- The chief instructor, assistant chief instructor, or the designated check instructor will evaluate the student's proficiency to determine if he/she is prepared to depart the traffic pattern area on future solo flights.
- In addition, the student will be evaluated in all other maneuvers, procedures, and knowledge areas appropriate to the first stage of the Flight Training Syllabus.

PREFLIGHT DISCUSSION:

CONDUCT OF THE STAGE I CHECK, INCLUDING:

❏ Maneuvers

❏ Procedures

❏ Acceptable performance criteria

❏ Applicable rules

REVIEW:

❏ Operation of Systems

❏ Minimum Equipment List

❏ Engine Starting

❏ Radio Communications

❏ Taxiing

❏ Before Takeoff Check

❏ Normal and/or Crosswind Takeoff and Climb

❏ Collision Avoidance Precautions

❏ Wake Turbulence Avoidance

❏ Maneuvering During Slow Flight

❏ Flight at Slow Airspeeds with Realistic Distractions, and the Recognition and Recovery from Stalls Entered from Straight Flight and from Turns

❏ Spin Awareness

❏ Power-Off Stalls

❏ Power-On Stalls

❏ Systems and Equipment Malfunctions

- ❏ Emergency Procedures
- ❏ Emergency Descent
- ❏ Emergency Approach and Landing
- ❏ Traffic Patterns
- ❏ Normal and/or Crosswind Approach and Landing

POSTFLIGHT DISCUSSION AND PREVIEW OF NEXT LESSON

STUDY ASSIGNMENT:

PRIVATE PILOT MANEUVERS —
Performance Takeoffs and Landings

←

STAGE II

STAGE OBJECTIVES

This stage allows the student to expand the skills learned in the previous stage. The student is introduced to short-field and soft-field takeoff and landing procedures, as well as night flying, which are important steps in preparation for cross-country training. Additionally, greater emphasis is placed on attitude control by instrument reference to increase the student's overall competence. In the cross-country phase, the student will learn to plan and conduct cross-country flights using pilotage, dead reckoning, and radio navigation systems, and how to safely conduct flights in the National Airspace System.

STAGE COMPLETION STANDARDS

This stage is complete when the student can accurately plan and conduct cross-country flights. In addition, the student will have the proficiency to safely demonstrate consistent results in performing short-field and soft-field takeoffs and landings and night operations. The proficiency level must be such that the successful and safe outcome of each task is never seriously in doubt.

STAGE II
FLIGHT LESSON 11
DUAL — LOCAL (1.0)

LESSON REFERENCES

PRIVATE PILOT MANEUVERS —
Performance Takeoffs and Landings

MANEUVERS VIDEO — Performance
Takeoffs and Landings

LESSON OBJECTIVES:
- Learn the basic procedures for short- and soft-field takeoffs, climbs, approaches, and landings in the training airplane.
- Review ground reference maneuvers, slow flight, and stall recognition.
- Determine if the student is competent to fly the second supervised solo in the traffic pattern.
- Emphasis on short- and soft-field takeoffs and landings.

PREFLIGHT DISCUSSION:
❏ Weight and balance computations
❏ Performance estimates
❏ Effects of high density altitude
❏ Aeronautical decision making
❏ Pilot-in-command responsibility

INTRODUCE:
❏ Low-Level Wind Shear Precautions
❏ Short-Field Takeoff and Climb
❏ Soft-Field Takeoff and Climb
❏ Short-Field Approach and Landing
❏ Soft-Field Approach and Landing

REVIEW.

- ❏ Rectangular Courses
- ❏ Turns Around a Point
- ❏ S-Turns
- ❏ Maneuvering During Slow Flight
- ❏ Flight at Slow Airspeeds with Realistic Distractions, and the Recognition and Recovery from Stalls Entered from Straight Flight and from Turns

POSTFLIGHT DISCUSSION AND PREVIEW OF NEXT LESSON

STUDY ASSIGNMENT:

Review, as required, in preparation for Flight Lesson 12, which is the second supervised solo in the traffic pattern.

COMPLETION STANDARDS:

- The student will be able to explain runway conditions that necessitate the use of soft-field and short-field takeoff and landing techniques.
- Demonstrate the correct procedure to be used under existing or simulated conditions, although proficiency may not be at private pilot level.
- Ground track during the ground reference maneuvers will be accurate. Maintain altitude ± 150 feet.

STAGE II
FLIGHT LESSON 12
SOLO— LOCAL (1.0)

Note: At the instructor's prerogative, a portion of this lesson may be dual.

LESSON OBJECTIVES:

* The student will fly the second supervised solo in the local traffic pattern.
* Emphasize airport operations, including takeoff, traffic pattern, approach and landing procedures, as well as collision avoidance and radio communications.

PREFLIGHT DISCUSSION:

❏ Solo operations in the traffic pattern

REVIEW:

SUPERVISED SOLO

❏ Radio Communications
❏ Taxiing
❏ Before Takeoff Check
❏ Normal Takeoff and Climb
❏ Traffic Patterns
❏ Normal Approach and Landing
❏ After Landing Procedures
❏ Parking and Securing

POSTFLIGHT DISCUSSION AND
PREVIEW OF NEXT LESSON

Review, as required, in preparation for the first solo flight in the local flying area.

- The student will perform each of the takeoffs using the correct techniques. Liftoff speed will not vary from the recommended speed by more than five knots.
- The landing approaches will be stabilized, and the approach speed will not vary more than five knots from the desired speed.
- Smooth landing touchdowns at the correct speed within 300 feet of the desired touchdown point.

STAGE II
FLIGHT LESSON 13
Solo — Local (1.0)

Lesson Objectives:
- Practice the listed maneuvers to gain proficiency and confidence.
- Review ground reference maneuvers to increase skill in maintaining specific ground tracks.
- Practice other maneuvers as directed by the flight instructor.
- Emphasis on traffic pattern entry, exit, approach, and landing procedures, including use of a stabilized approach.

Review:
❏ Radio Communications
❏ Normal and/or Crosswind Takeoffs and Climbs
❏ Power-Off Stalls
❏ Power-On Stalls
❏ Maneuvering During Slow Flight
❏ S-Turns
❏ Turns Around a Point
❏ Traffic Patterns
❏ Normal and/or Crosswind Approaches and Landings

PRIVATE PILOT MANEUVERS —
Attitude Instrument Flying

←

STAGE II
FLIGHT LESSON 14
DUAL — LOCAL (1.0)

Note: A view-limiting device is required for the .5 hour of dual instrument time allocated to Flight Lesson 14.

LESSON REFERENCES

PRIVATE PILOT MANEUVERS —
Attitude Instrument Flying

MANEUVERS VIDEO — Attitude
Instrument Flying

LESSON OBJECTIVES:

• Practice the listed maneuvers to gain proficiency and confidence.
• Introduce airplane control by instrument reference during emergency situations to broaden the student's knowledge.
• Emphasis will be on the introduction of VOR and ADF orientation, tracking, and homing, as well as attitude instrument flying.

PREFLIGHT DISCUSSION:

❏ Basic instrument maneuvers, including recovery from unusual flight attitudes
❏ Radio communication, navigation systems/facilities, and radar services
❏ Emergency descents and climbs
❏ Resource use
❏ Situational Awareness
❏ Disorientation

INTRODUCE:

❏ VOR Orientation and Tracking (VR)
❏ ADF Orientation and Homing (VR)
❏ Power-Off Stalls (IR)
❏ Power-On Stalls (IR)

❏ Recovery from Unusual Flight Attitudes
❏ Emergency Descents and Climbs using Radio Aids or Radar Directives (IR)
❏ Using Radio Communications, Navigation Systems/Facilities, and Radar Services (IR)

REVIEW:
❏ Low Level Wind Shear Precautions
❏ Short-Field Takeoffs and Climbs
❏ Short-Field Approaches and Landings
❏ Power-Off Stalls
❏ Power-On Stalls
❏ Maneuvering During Slow Flight (IR)

POSTFLIGHT DISCUSSION AND PREVIEW OF NEXT LESSON

COMPLETION STANDARDS:

- Perform takeoffs and landings smoothly, while maintaining good directional control. Approaches will be stabilized, and airspeed will be within five knots of that desired.

- Demonstrate basic understanding of VOR/ADF orientation, tracking and homing.

- Display the correct unusual attitude recovery techniques and be able to initiate emergency climbs and descents by instrument reference using radio communications, navigation facilities, and radar services.

STAGE II
FLIGHT LESSON 15
DUAL — LOCAL INSTRUMENT (1.0)

Note: A view-limiting device is required for the .5 hour of dual instrument time allocated to Flight Lesson 15.

LESSON OBJECTIVES:

- Review attitude instrument flying, including all instrument procedures intended to help a private pilot (without an instrument rating) avoid hazardous situations due to marginal VMC or inadvertent flight into IMC.
- Review short- and soft-field procedures and emergency operations.
- Emphasis on attitude instrument flying.

PREFLIGHT DISCUSSION:

❑ Flight instrument functions, common errors, and limitations
❑ Navigation instruments
❑ Inadvertent flight into IMC
❑ Operations in turbulence
❑ Partial panel
❑ Resource use

REVIEW:

❑ VOR Orientation and Tracking (VR-IR)
❑ ADF Orientation and Homing (VR-IR)
❑ Flight on Federal Airways
❑ Maneuvering During Slow Flight (VR-IR)
❑ Power-Off Stalls (VR-IR)
❑ Power-On Stalls (VR-IR)
❑ Emergency Descents and Climbs using Radio Aids or Radar Directives (IR)
❑ Using Radio Communication, Navigation Systems/Facilities, and Radar Services (IR)
❑ Recovery From Unusual Flight Attitudes (IR)
❑ Short-Field Takeoffs and Landings
❑ Soft-Field Takeoffs and Landings
❑ Crosswind Takeoffs and Landings
❑ Forward Slips to a Landing
❑ Go-Around
❑ Emergency Operations

STUDY ASSIGNMENT:

PRIVATE PILOT MANEUVERS —
Night Operations

COMPLETION STANDARDS:

- Demonstrate competency in basic instrument maneuvers and procedures at the private pilot level, including control of the airplane during unusual attitude recoveries, and emergency climbs and descents.

- Control altitude ± 150 feet during level turns, straight-and-level flight, and slow flight. Stall recoveries should be coordinated with a minimum loss of altitude.

- Demonstrate increasing skill in short- and soft-field takeoff and landing procedures.

- Display the correct recovery techniques from stalls and unusual attitudes.

- Be able to initiate emergency climbs and descents by instrument reference using radio communications, navigation facilities, and radar services.

STAGE II
FLIGHT LESSON 16
DUAL — NIGHT LOCAL (1.0)

LESSON REFERENCES:

 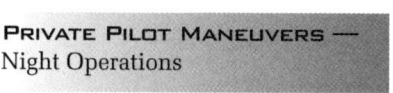

PRIVATE PILOT MANEUVERS — Night Operations

MANEUVERS VIDEO — Night Operations

LESSON OBJECTIVES:

- Introduce the special operational considerations associated with night flying.
- Practice night traffic patterns, approaches, and landings.
- Stress importance of including instrument references for maintaining attitude.
- Emphasize the physiological factors and additional planning associated with the night environment.

PREFLIGHT DISCUSSION:

❑ Preparation for night flying
❑ Night vision
❑ Disorientation
❑ Visual illusions
❑ Night scanning/collision avoidance
❑ Aircraft, airport, and obstruction lighting
❑ Personal equipment

INTRODUCE:

❑ Aeromedical Factors
❑ Flight Planning Considerations
❑ Use of Checklists
❑ Preflight Inspection
❑ Minimum Equipment List
❑ Taxiing

- ❑ ~~Before Takeoff Check~~
- ❑ Power-Off Stalls
- ❑ Power-On Stalls
- ❑ Steep Turns
- ❑ Maneuvering During Slow Flight
- ❑ Normal Takeoffs and Climbs
- ❑ Normal Approaches and Landings
- ❑ Short-Field Takeoffs and Landings
- ❑ Soft-Field Takeoffs and Landings
- ❑ Go-Around
- ❑ VFR Navigation

STUDY ASSIGNMENT:

Review, as required, in preparation for the dual cross-country in Flight Lesson 17.

POSTFLIGHT DISCUSSION AND PREVIEW OF NEXT LESSON

NOTE: *The 10 night takeoffs and landings to a full stop with each involving flight in the traffic pattern are an FAR Part 141 requirement. Five are scheduled for Flight Lesson 16 and the other five for Flight Lesson 18. However, this requirement may be accomplished with fewer than five during a flight, as long as the total of 10 is completed.*

COMPLETION STANDARDS:

- Demonstrate an understanding of the importance of attitude control.
- Control altitude ± 150 feet during level turns, straight-and-level flight, and slow flight. Stall recoveries should be coordinated with a minimum loss of altitude.
- Complete 5 takeoffs and landings to a full stop with each landing involving flight in the traffic pattern.
- All landing approaches should be stabilized with touchdown at a predetermined area on the runway.

STAGE II
FLIGHT LESSON 17
DUAL — CROSS-COUNTRY (2.0)

Note: A view-limiting device is required for the .5 hour of dual instrument time allocated to Flight Lesson 17.

LESSON OBJECTIVES:

• Introduce cross-country procedures and the proper techniques to be used during flights out of the local training area, including use of VOR, ADF, and radar services under simulated instrument flight conditions.

• Prepare the student to make cross-country flights as the sole occupant of the airplane.

• Review instrument and emergency operations.

• Emphasize cross-country navigation procedures that include a point of landing at ◄— least a straight-line distance of more than 50 nautical miles from the original point of departure.

PREFLIGHT DISCUSSION:

CROSS-COUNTRY FLIGHT PLANNING

❏ Sectional charts
❏ Flight publications
❏ Route selection and basic navigation procedures (pilotage and dead reckoning)
❏ Weather information
❏ Fuel requirements
❏ Performance and limitations
❏ Navigation log
❏ FAA flight plan (how to open, close, or amend)
❏ Weight and balance
❏ Cockpit management
❏ Aeromedical factors
❏ Aeronautical decision making
❏ Resource use
❏ Workload management
❏ Basic instrument maneuvers and procedures

INTRODUCE:

CROSS-COUNTRY FLIGHT

❏ Departure
❏ Opening Flight Plan

- Course Interception
- Pilotage
- Dead Reckoning
- VOR Navigation
- ADF Navigation
- Power Settings and Mixture Control
- Diversion to an Alternate
- Lost Procedures
- Estimates of Groundspeed and ETA
- Position Fix by Navigation Facilities
- Flight on Federal Airways
- Collision Avoidance Precautions
- Closing the Flight Plan

INSTRUMENT FLIGHT
- VOR Tracking (IR)
- ADF Homing (IR)
- Use of Radar Services (IR)

AIRPORT OPERATIONS
- National Airspace System
- Controlled Airports
- Use of ATIS
- Use of Approach and Departure Control
- Go-Arounds
- CTAF (FSS or UNICOM) Airports

REVIEW:
- Emergency Operations
- Systems and Equipment Malfunctions
- Emergency Descent
- Runway Incursion Avoidance
- Emergency Approach and Landing
- Emergency Equipment and Survival Gear

POSTFLIGHT DISCUSSION AND PREVIEW OF NEXT LESSON

COMPLETION STANDARDS:

- Demonstrate the skill to perform cross-country flight safely as the sole occupant of the airplane, including use of navigation systems and radar services under simulated instrument conditions.

- Include a point of landing at least a straight-line distance of more than 50 nautical miles from the original point of departure.

- Demonstrate complete preflight planning, weather analysis, use of FAA publications and charts, adherence to the preflight plan, and the use of pilotage, dead reckoning, radio communication, and navigation systems.

STAGE II
FLIGHT LESSON 18
DUAL — NIGHT CROSS-COUNTRY (2.0)

Note: A view-limiting device is required for the .5 hour of dual instrument time allocated to Flight Lesson 18.

LESSON OBJECTIVES:

- Introduce night navigation and emergency operations.
- Recognize the importance of thorough planning and accurate navigation.
- The flight should include a total distance of more than 100 nautical miles and a point of landing at least a straight-line distance of more than 50 nautical miles from the original point of departure.
- Attitude instrument flying practice.
- Emphasize precise aircraft control and the navigation accuracy required for night VFR cross-country flights.

PREFLIGHT DISCUSSION:

❑ Night orientation, navigation, and chart reading techniques
❑ Weather information
❑ Route selection
❑ Altitude selection
❑ Fuel requirements
❑ Departure and arrival procedures

INTRODUCE:

❑ Use of ATIS, Approach, and Departure Control
❑ Pilotage
❑ Dead Reckoning
❑ Radio Navigation (VR-IR)
❑ Emergency Operations
❑ Use of Unfamiliar Airports
❑ Collision Avoidance Precautions
❑ Diversion to Alternate
❑ Lost Procedures
❑ Unusual Attitude Recoveries (IR)

REVIEW:

❑ Aeromedical Factors
❑ Maneuvering During Slow Flight (VR-IR)
❑ Normal Takeoffs and Climbs
❑ Normal Approaches and Landings
❑ Short-Field Takeoffs and Landings
❑ Soft-Field Takeoffs and Landings
❑ Go-Around

POSTFLIGHT DISCUSSION AND PREVIEW OF NEXT LESSON

STUDY ASSIGNMENT:

Prepare for the Solo Cross-Country Briefing.

COMPLETION STANDARDS:

• Demonstrate an understanding of night cross-country preparation and flight procedures, including ability to maintain attitude by instrument reference.

• Navigation should be accurate, and simulated emergency situations should be handled promptly, utilizing proper judgment.

• Total distance of more than 100 nautical miles required.

• In addition, the flight must include a point of landing at least a straight-line distance of more than 50 nautical miles from the original point of departure.

• Complete 5 takeoffs and landings to a full stop with each involving flight in the traffic pattern.

• Landing approaches stabilized with touchdown at or near the appropriate touchdown area on the runway.

FLIGHT LESSONS

STAGE II
FLIGHT LESSON 19
SOLO — CROSS-COUNTRY (2.5)

LESSON OBJECTIVES:
- Use previous experience and training to complete solo cross country.
- Increase proficiency and confidence.
- The flight should include a point of landing that is at least a straight-line distance of more than 50 nautical miles from the original point of departure.
- Emphasize planning and following the plan, including alternatives.

PREFLIGHT DISCUSSION:
❏ Review the Solo Cross-Country Briefing
❏ Required documents and endorsements
❏ Basic VFR weather minimums and airspace rules
❏ Enroute communication
❏ ATC services available to pilots
❏ Enroute weather information
❏ VFR position report
❏ Emergency operations
❏ Lost procedures
❏ Diversion
❏ Lost communication procedures
❏ ATC light signals
❏ Aeronautical decision making
❏ Resource use
❏ Workload management

REVIEW:

PREFLIGHT PREPARATION
❏ Sectional Charts
❏ Flight Publications
❏ Route Selection
❏ Weather Information
❏ Fuel Requirements
❏ Performance and Limitations
❏ Weight and Balance
❏ Navigation Log

❏ FAA Flight Plan
❏ Aeromedical Factors

CROSS-COUNTRY FLIGHT
❏ Opening the Flight Plan
❏ VOR and ADF Navigation
❏ Position Fix by Navigation Facilities
❏ Pilotage
❏ Dead Reckoning
❏ Use of Unfamiliar Airports
❏ Estimates of Groundspeed
❏ Estimates of ETA
❏ Closing the Flight Plan

POSTFLIGHT DISCUSSION AND PREVIEW OF NEXT LESSON

STUDY ASSIGNMENT:

Review as required in preparation for the Stage II Check in Flight Lesson 20.

COMPLETION STANDARDS:

- Demonstrate accurate planning and conduct of a VFR cross-country flight using the three methods of navigation.
- During the postflight evaluation, the student will exhibit an understanding of unfamiliar airport operations.
- At least one landing more than 50 n.m. from the departure airport.

STAGE II
FLIGHT LESSON 20
DUAL — LOCAL (1.0)
STAGE CHECK

LESSON OBJECTIVES:

* This stage check, conducted by the chief instructor, the assistant chief instructor, or the designated check instructor, will evaluate the student's takeoff, landing, and stall recognition/recovery procedures to determine any areas of weakness.
* Additionally, the student's ability to plan and conduct cross-country flights will be evaluated, as well as safe and effective operation of the aircraft during all other phases of flight in Stages I and II of the Private Pilot Flight Training Syllabus.

PREFLIGHT DISCUSSION:

CONDUCT OF THE STAGE II CHECK, INCLUDING:
❏ Maneuvers
❏ Procedures
❏ Acceptable performance criteria
❏ Applicable rules

REVIEW:

PREFLIGHT PREPARATION
❏ National Airspace System
❏ Cross-Country Planning
❏ Weather Information
❏ Cockpit Management
❏ Use of Checklists

CROSS-COUNTRY FLIGHT
❏ Departure
❏ Course Interception
❏ VOR Navigation
❏ Pilotage
❏ Dead Reckoning
❏ Collision Avoidance Precautions
❏ Low Level Wind Shear Precautions
❏ Diversion to Alternate
❏ Lost Procedures
❏ Emergency Operations

❑ Use of Power Settings and Mixture Control
❑ Soft-Field Takeoffs and Climbs
❑ Soft-Field Approaches and Landings
❑ Short-Field Takeoffs and Climbs
❑ Short-Field Approaches and Landings
❑ Power-Off Stalls
❑ Power-On Stalls

POSTFLIGHT DISCUSSION AND PREVIEW OF NEXT LESSON

COMPLETION STANDARDS:

- Demonstrate the ability to plan and conduct cross-country flights using sound knowledge of flight planning, preflight action, weather analysis, and the appropriate aeronautical publications.

- Exhibit the correct use of three methods of navigation, the ability to correctly determine location at any time, the ability to compute ETAs within 10 minutes, and the correct technique for establishing a course to an alternate airport.

- Demonstrate short- and soft-field takeoffs and landings safely with consistent results.

- The student should be proficient in all other maneuvers and procedures, as well as the associated knowledge area of Stages I and II prior to advancing to Stage III.

STAGE III

STAGE OBJECTIVES

During this stage, the student will gain additional proficiency in solo cross-country operations and will receive instruction in preparation for the End-of-Course Flight Check.

STAGE COMPLETION STANDARDS

This stage will be complete when the student demonstrates performance of private pilot operations at a standard that meets or exceeds the minimum performance criteria established in the practical test standards for a private pilot certificate.

STAGE III
FLIGHT LESSON 21
Solo — Cross-Country (2.0)   ←

Lesson Objectives:
- Complete the scheduled cross-country flight to improve judgment and confidence when operating in unfamiliar areas.
- The flight should include a point of landing at least a straight-line distance of more than 50 nautical miles from the original point of departure.
- Three takeoffs and landings to a full stop with each landing involving flight in the traffic pattern at an airport with an operating control tower.
- Emphasize cross-country procedures and rules for flight within Class D airspace.

Preflight Discussion:
❑ Required documents and endorsements
❑ Basic VFR weather minimums
❑ Route of flight/alternates, emergency operations
❑ Lost procedures
❑ Diversion
❑ ETA estimates
❑ Fuel requirements
❑ Aeronautical charts and publications that apply to the flgiht
❑ Airspace rules pertinent to the planned route of flight
❑ Enroute communication, ATC services, and pertinent sources of weather information
❑ Aeronautical decision making
❑ Situational awareness

Review:

Preflight Preparation
❑ Sectional Charts
❑ Flight Publications
❑ Route Selection
❑ Weather Information
❑ Fuel Requirements
❑ Performance and Limitations
❑ Weight and Balance
❑ Navigation Log
❑ FAA Flight Plan

- ❏ VOR Navigation
- ❏ Position Fix by Navigation Facilities
- ❏ Pilotage
- ❏ Dead Reckoning
- ❏ Estimates of Groundspeed
- ❏ Estimates of ETA
- ❏ Use of Unfamiliar Airports

POSTFLIGHT DISCUSSION AND PREVIEW OF NEXT LESSON

NOTE: *The solo training requirement for three takeoffs, landings, and traffic patterns at a controlled airport may be completed in other flight lessons. This is a private pilot certification requirement which does not necessarily have to be accomplished during a specific flight lesson.*

COMPLETION STANDARDS:

- This lesson is complete when the student has conducted the assigned cross-country flight.
- Review the student's navigation log; revised in-flight ETAs at each checkpoint should not vary from the ATAs by more than ± 5 minutes.
- At least one landing more than 50 n.m. from the departure airport.
- * Successfully accomplish the three traffic pattern, takeoff, and landing requirements at a controlled aiport.

STAGE III
FLIGHT LESSON 22
SOLO — CROSS-COUNTRY (4.0)

LESSON OBJECTIVES:
- During this lesson, the student will complete the long cross-country requirement.
- This flight should be of at least 100 nautical miles, total distance, with landings at a minimum of three points, including a straight-line segment at least 50 nautical miles between takeoff and landing locations.
- Three takeoffs and landings to a full stop with each landing involving flight in the traffic pattern at an airport with an operating control tower.
- Emphasize cross-country procedures and rules for flight within Class D airspace.

PREFLIGHT DISCUSSION:
❏ Conduct of the planned flight
❏ Cockpit management, decision making, and judgment
❏ FAA flight plan (how to open, close, or amend)
❏ Use of the magnetic compass
❏ Emergency descent procedures
❏ Emergency operations
❏ Enroute communications and facilities
❏ In-flight weather analysis
❏ Unfamiliar airport operations

REVIEW:

PREFLIGHT PREPARATION
❏ National Airspace System
❏ Sectional Charts
❏ Flight Publications
❏ Route Selection
❏ Weather Information
❏ Fuel Requirements
❏ Performance and Limitations
❏ Weight and Balance
❏ Navigation Log
❏ FAA Flight Plan

- ❑ Opening and Closing the Flight Plan
- ❑ VOR Navigation
- ❑ Pilotage
- ❑ Dead Reckoning
- ❑ Estimates of Groundspeed
- ❑ Estimates of ETA
- ❑ Use of Controlled Airports
- ❑ Use of Airports with CTAF (FSS and/or UNICOM)

POSTFLIGHT DISCUSSION AND PREVIEW OF NEXT LESSON

COMPLETION STANDARDS:

NOTE: *Due to the amount of time needed to complete this cross-country flight, the lesson may be conducted as two flights. If this is done, and in order for the flight to be classified as cross country, each flight must include a landing more than 50 n.m. from the departure airport.*

In addition, the requirement for three takeoffs, landings, and traffic patterns at a controlled airport may be completed in other flight lessons. This is a private pilot certification requirement which does not necessarily have to be accomplished during a specific flight lesson.

- Demonstrate cross-country proficiency by completing the flight as planned and without incident.
- Review the completed navigation log during the postflight evaluation to determine whether it was completed and used correctly.
- The cross-country flight must include a distance of over 100 n.m. with landings at a minimum of three points, including at least one segment of the flight consisting of a straight-line distance of at least 50 n.m. between takeoff and landing locations.
- Successfully accomplish the three traffic pattern, takeoff, and landing requirements at a controlled airport.

STAGE III
FLIGHT LESSON 23
DUAL — LOCAL (2.0)

LESSON OBJECTIVES:

* Review the areas of operation, including specified maneuvers and procedures determined by the instructor to increase proficiency to the level required of a private pilot.
* Further develop the student's knowledge and skill in preparation for the private pilot practical test.
* Emphasis will be on correction of any deficient skill or knowledge areas.

PREFLIGHT DISCUSSION:

❏ Maneuvers and procedures in preparation for the Stage III Check, End-of-Course Flight Check, and FAA Practical Test, including spin awareness and night operations.

REVIEW:

❏ Preflight Preparation
❏ Ground Operations
❏ Maneuvering During Slow Flight (VR-IR)
❏ Power-Off and Power-On Stalls (VR-IR)
❏ Steep Turns
❏ Ground Reference Maneuvers
❏ Emergency Descents and Climbs Using Radio Aids or Radar Directives (IR)
❏ Using Radio Communications, Navigation Systems/Facilities, and Radar Services (IR)
❏ Unusual Attitude Recoveries (IR)
❏ Airport Operations
❏ Normal and/or Crosswind Takeoffs and Landings
❏ Go-Around from a Rejected Landing
❏ Short-Field Takeoffs and Landings
❏ Soft-Field Takeoffs and Landings
❏ Forward Slips to Landing
❏ Emergency Operations
❏ After Landing Procedures
❏ Parking and Securing the Airplane
❏ Cross-Country Flight Procedures
❏ Specific Maneuvers or Procedures Assigned by the Flight Instructor

COMPLETION STANDARDS:

* The student will exhibit progress and acceptable proficiency by performing each assigned maneuver smoothly and with proper coordination and precision according to the criteria established by the Private Pilot Practical Test Standards.

(7/99)

STAGE III
FLIGHT LESSON 24
DUAL — LOCAL (2.0)

LESSON OBJECTIVES:
- Review the areas of operation specifically assigned by the instructor with special emphasis on correcting any deficiency in the performance of maneuvers or procedures before the Stage III Check.
- Further develop the student's knowledge and skill in preparation for the private pilot practical test.
- Emphasis will be on correction of any deficient skill or knowledge areas.

PREFLIGHT DISCUSSION:
❑ Maneuvers and procedures in preparation for the Stage III Check, End-of-Course Flight Check and FAA Practical Test, inclucing spin awareness and night operations

REVIEW:
❑ Preflight Preparation
❑ Ground Operations
❑ Maneuvering During Slow Flight (VR-IR)
❑ Power-Off and Power-On Stalls (VR-IR)
❑ Steep Turns
❑ Ground Reference Maneuvers
❑ Emergency Descents and Climbs Using Radio Aids or Radar Directives (IR)
❑ Using Radio Communications, Navigation Systems/Facilities, and Radar Services (IR)
❑ Unusual Attitude Recoveries (IR)
❑ Airport Operations
❑ Normal and/or Crosswind Takeoffs and Landings
❑ Go-Around from a Rejected Landing
❑ Short-Field Takeoffs and Landings
❑ Soft-Field Takeoffs and Landings
❑ Forward Slips to Landing
❑ Emergency Operations
❑ After Landing Procedures
❑ Parking and Securing the Airplane
❑ Cross-Country Flight Procedures
❑ Specific Maneuvers or Procedures Assigned by the Flight Instructor

COMPLETION STANDARDS:
- The lesson is complete when the student has practiced the assigned maneuvers and procedures.
- The student should exhibit competence and abiltiy to correct any weak performance areas determined previously.
- Perform each assigned maneuver and procedure with proper coordination and precision according to the criteria established in the Private Pilot Practical Test Standards.

POSTFLIGHT DISCUSSION AND PREVIEW OF NEXT LESSON

STAGE III
FLIGHT LESSON 25
DUAL — LOCAL (1.0)
STAGE CHECK

LESSON OBJECTIVES:
- This stage check, conducted by the chief instructor, the assistant chief instructor, or the designated check instructor, will evaluate the student's ability to perform the listed maneuvers at the proficiency level of a private pilot.
- Additionally, the student's ability to plan and conduct cross-country flights safely will be evaluated, as well as safe and effective operation of the aircraft during all other phases of flight in Stage III of the Private Pilot Flight Training Syllabus.

PREFLIGHT DISCUSSION:
CONDUCT OF THE STAGE III CHECK, INCLUDING:
❑ Maneuvers
❑ Procedures
❑ Acceptable performance criteria
❑ Applicable rules
❑ Human factors concepts

REVIEW:
MANEUVERS AND PROCEDURES
❑ Preflight Preparation
❑ Ground Operations
❑ Maneuvering During Slow Flight (VR-IR)
❑ Power-Off and Power-On Stalls (VR-IR)
❑ Steep Turns
❑ Ground Reference Maneuvers
❑ Emergency Descents and Climbs Using Radio Aids or Radar Directives (IR)
❑ Using Radio Communications, Navigation Systems/Facilities, and Radar Services (IR)
❑ Unusual Attitude Recoveries (IR)
❑ Airport Operations
❑ Normal and/or Crosswind Takeoffs and Landings
❑ Go-Around from a Rejected Landing
❑ Short-Field Takeoffs and Landings
❑ Soft-Field Takeoffs and Landings
❑ Forward Slips to Landing
❑ Emergency Operations
❑ After Landing Procedures
❑ Parking and Securing the Airplane

❏ Radio Navigation
❏ Pilotage and Dead Reckoning
❏ Diversion to Alternate
❏ Lost Procedures

POSTFLIGHT DISCUSSION AND
PREVIEW OF NEXT LESSON

STUDY ASSIGNMENT:

Private Pilot Practical Test Briefing in preparation for the End-of-Course Flight Check and the FAA Practical Test.

COMPLETION STANDARDS:

- Each maneuver and procedure should be performed at the proficiency level of a private pilot.

- Mastery of the airplane should be evident and the successful outcome of each task performed should be expected.

- Any maneuvers or procedures which do not meet this standard should be reviewed with the student and assigned additional practice.

- Student should exhibit a sound understanding of the knowledge, skill, and proficiency requirements for private pilot certification.

- Demonstrate the ability to plan and conduct cross-country flights using sound knowledge of flight planning, preflight action, weather analysis, and the appropriate aeronautical publications.

STAGE III
FLIGHT LESSON 26
DUAL — LOCAL (1.0)
END-OF-COURSE FLIGHT CHECK

LESSON OBJECTIVES:
• This End-of-Course Flight Check, conducted by the chief instructor, the assistant chief instructor, or the designated check instructor, is to evaluate the student's overall proficiency, skill, and knowledge in private pilot operations.

• Additionally, the student will exhibit the sound judgment and decision making capabilities necessary for a private pilot to operate effectively and safely within the U.S. National Airspace System.

PREFLIGHT DISCUSSION:
CONDUCT OF THE END-OF-COURSE FLIGHT CHECK, INCLUDING:
❑ Maneuvers
❑ Procedures
❑ Acceptable performance criteria
❑ Applicable rules

REVIEW:
PREFLIGHT PREPARATION
❑ Certificates and Documents
❑ Weather Information
❑ Performance and Limitations
❑ Cross-Country Flight Planning
❑ Operation of Systems
❑ Aeromedical Factors

CROSS-COUNTRY FLYING
❑ Pilotage and Dead Reckoning
❑ Radio Navigation
❑ Diversion to an Alternate
❑ Lost Procedures

BASIC PILOTING SKILLS
❑ Preflight Inspection
❑ Cockpit Management
❑ Use of Checklist
❑ Engine Starting

- Taxiing
- Before Takeoff Check
- Radio Communications
- ATC Light Signals
- Collision Avoidance Precautions
- Low-Level Wind Shear Precautions
- Wake Turbulence Avoidance
- Airport and Runway Markings and Lighting
- Normal and Crosswind Takeoffs and Climbs
- Short-Field Takeoff and Climb
- Soft-Field Takeoff and Climb
- Straight-and-Level Flight (VR-IR)
- Constant Airspeed Climbs (VR-IR)
- Constant Airspeed Descents (VR-IR)
- Turns to Headings (VR-IR)
- Unusual Attitudes (IR)
- Using Radio Communications, Navigation Facilities, and Radar Services (IR)
- Maneuvering During Slow Flight
- Power-Off Stalls
- Power-On Stalls
- Flight at Slow Airspeeds with Realistic Distractions, and the Recognition and Recovery from Stalls Entered from Straight Flight and Turns
- Spin Awareness
- Steep Turns
- Ground Reference Maneuvers
- Emergency Descent
- Emergency Approach and Landing
- Emergency Equipment and Survival Gear
- Systems and Equipment Malfunctions
- Traffic Patterns
- Normal and Crosswind Approaches and Landings
- Forward Slips to Landing
- Go-Arounds
- Short-Field Approach and Landing
- Soft-Field Approach and Landing
- After Landing Procedures
- Parking and Securing

COMPLETION STANDARDS:

- The student will demonstrate proficiency that meets or exceeds the standard of performance outlined in the current FAA Private Pilot Practical Test Standards.
- Mastery of the airplane should be demonstrated with the successful outcome of each task performed never seriously in doubt.
- Additional instruction will be assigned, if necessary, to meet the stage and course completion standards.

This is to Certify that

_____

is enrolled in the

Federal Aviation Administration

approved _____ course

conducted by _____ .

Date of Enrollment _____

Chief Instructor _____

This is to certify that

_____

has succesfully completed all stages, tests, and
course requirements and has graduated from the
FEDERAL AVIATION ADMINISTRATION
approved _____ course
conducted by _____.

The graduate has completed the cross-country
training specified in FAR Part 141.

☐ Private Pilot Certification Course —
   Appendix B, Paragraphs 4 and 5

☐ Instrument Rating Course — Appendix C,
   Paragraph 4(c)(1)(ii)

☐ Commercial Pilot Certification Course —
   Appendix D, Paragraphs 4 and 5

☐ Other: _____
   _____

I certify the above statements are true.

_____
Chief Instructor

_____
School certificate number

_____
Date of graduation